Foundations of BizTalk Server 2006

■ ■ ■

Daniel Woolston

Apress®

Foundations of BizTalk Server 2006

Copyright © 2007 by Daniel Woolston

ISBN-13 (pbk): 978-1-59059-775-0

ISBN-10 (pbk): 1-59059-775-3

Printed and bound in the United States of America 9 8 7 6 5 4 3 2 1

Lead Editor: Jonathan Hassell
Technical Reviewer: Stephen Kaufman
Editorial Board: Steve Anglin, Ewan Buckingham, Gary Cornell, Jason Gilmore, Jonathan Gennick,
    Jonathan Hassell, James Huddleston, Chris Mills, Matthew Moodie, Dominic Shakeshaft, Jim Sumser,
    Keir Thomas, Matt Wade
Project Manager: Elizabeth Seymour
Copy Edit Manager: Nicole Flores
Copy Editor: Marilyn Smith
Assistant Production Director: Kari Brooks-Copony
Production Editor: Laura Cheu
Compositor: Patrick Cunningham
Proofreader: Dan Shaw
Indexer: Tim Tate
Artist: April Milne
Cover Designer: Kurt Krames
Manufacturing Director: Tom Debolski

Distributed to the book trade worldwide by Springer-Verlag New York, Inc., 233 Spring Street, 6th Floor, New York, NY 10013. Phone 1-800-SPRINGER, fax 201-348-4505, e-mail orders-ny@springer-sbm.com, or visit http://www.springeronline.com.

For information on translations, please contact Apress directly at 2560 Ninth Street, Suite 219, Berkeley, CA 94710. Phone 510-549-5930, fax 510-549-5939, e-mail info@apress.com, or visit http://www.apress.com.

Dedicated to Michelle, Aymee, and Michael.
Without the group hugs, funny faces, goofy dances, fart jokes, and an occasional
impromptu mooning, my life would be empty and meaningless. You've given me balance
and happiness beyond compare.

Contents at a Glance

Contents

        Creating the Schema Project 121
        Creating the Pipeline Project 123
        Testing the Pipelines Project 128
    Summary. 133

■CHAPTER 10 **Orchestrations** 135

    What Is an Orchestration? 135
    Introducing the Orchestration Designer 136
    Building the Application 139
        Building the Orchestration 141
        Deploying the Application. 146
        Configuring and Starting the Application. 146
    Summary. 152

■CHAPTER 11 **Advanced Orchestrations** 153

    Correlation 153
        Understanding Dehydration and Persistence Points 154
        Building the Correlation Application 155
        Testing the Correlation Application. 166
    Failed Messages 169
        Creating an Application with Routable Errors 169
        Building the Handler Application 171
        Testing the Handler Application 175
    Summary. 176

■CHAPTER 12 **Business Rules** 177

    What Is the Business Rules Engine? 177
        Business Rules. 178
        Forward-Chaining Processes. 178
    Introducing the Business Rule Composer 179
        Policy Explorer 180
        Facts Explorer. 180
        Properties Window. 182
        Policy Instructions Window 183
    Implementing a Business Rule 183
        Creating a Business Rule Application. 184
        Creating a Business Rule 188
        Adding the Business Rule to the Orchestration 192

About the Author

Author Daniel Woolston with his wife, Michelle

DANIEL WOOLSTON is the President and Senior Developer for Integrated Coding Inc. of Grand Rapids, Michigan (http://www.integratedcoding.com). He is currently working with one of the largest online retailers on the planet, helping to develop the next generation of customer-focused applications.

Daniel's software journey began in the late 1980s with the infamous Sinclair ZX80. His current ambitions involve developing .NET-centric integration applications utilizing the latest technologies and beyond. His work efforts have branched from Fortune 500 enterprise application development to pattern-driven project implementations on various corporate levels. He has years of experience in designing and distributing VB/VB.NET/C#/BizTalk development projects. Daniel recently authored *Pro Ajax and the .Net 2.0 Platform* (available from Apress, http://www.apress.com).

When Daniel isn't knee-deep in code, he can typically be found at the local hockey rink watching the Grand Rapids Griffins stomp all who would dare to take the ice. Daniel also keeps a running blog at http://www.danwoolston.com.

About the Technical Reviewer

STEPHEN KAUFMAN is a Principal Consultant with Microsoft Consulting Services and has been working with BizTalk since the original BizTalk CTP in 1999. In addition, he is an author, trainer, and speaker. He has written Microsoft Knowledge Base articles, a BizTalk tools whitepaper, and a number of other articles. He was a contributing author for the BizTalk Certification Exam 74-135. Stephen has spoken nationally at events such as Microsoft Developer Days and TechEd, as well as at a number of other conferences. He writes a blog focused on integration technologies at http://blogs.msdn.com/skaufman.

Acknowledgments

This was quite possibly the hardest page in the book to write. There are so many people that have made a positive impact on my life as a developer and as a person. I'm desperately paranoid that I'll leave someone out that really should have been here and that ill feelings will ensue. If you're that person, please understand that it was an oversight and not an intention.

Without further ado, I would like to express my undying appreciation to the following for the various roles that they have played in molding this book and the author behind it:

Jim Wilt, for his unending passion for technology and willingness to pass that on to others. I'm deeply indebted to you for your mentoring and encouragement. (Website: `http://www.metricsreporting.com`)

Nick McCollum, for being an endless supply of knowledge and encouragement. (Website: `http://nickjmc.blogspot.com`)

Adrian Pavelescu, for never accepting mediocrity and pushing others to do the same. I am a better person and developer because of our friendship. (Website: `http://www.virtual-adrian.com`)

Ryan Smallegan, for his contagious desire to find the next big technology boom. (Website: `http://www.smallegan.com`)

Bruce Abernethy, for his unending sense of humor and his willingness to lend a helping hand. (Website: `http://brucesbanter.spaces.live.com`)

Mark Berry and Mark Dunn of Dunn Training, for an extraordinary training experience. They are, by far, the best training company that I have ever dealt with in my IT career.

The fantastic crew at Apress, Elizabeth Seymour, Marilyn Smith, Laura Cheu, Jon Hassell, Tina Nielsen, and Gary Cornell have all helped to make Apress the most developer-friendly publisher on the planet. Two books later, and I can't imagine writing for anyone else.

Tech editor Stephen Kaufman, who made this book stronger. It has been a pleasure working with you.

Steve and Arlene Ford, for always having a kind word and a warm home. Your faith and prayers have carried me when I was too weak to walk on my own.

My Mom and Dad, Terry and Cathy Woolston, for buying a home computer when no one else had one and for always being a phone call away.

Greg and Debbie Maroun, for helping to plant a seed that has grown into so much more.

Introduction

I have always been a fan of complexity. Some people fear and avoid it, but for some strange reason, I thrive on it. I'm a huge fan of puzzle games and typically have a Rubik's Cube well within reach to satiate my need for concentrated problem-solving. It's a strange obsession that many of you, my brothers and sisters in technology, share. We excel at coding and application integration because we feed on the detailed process by which we deliver our products. Many of the things that we accomplish may seem impossible at first, but numerous hours (and gallons of caffeine) later, we roll out a product or plan that we're proud to put our name on. And we do that because we love complexity.

I was drawn to BizTalk Server because I had heard many developers and architects say that the product was difficult to learn and had a deep level of intricacy. Few people were interested in learning the product, so I felt as if the gauntlet had been thrown. I told myself, "This truly is a product worth learning, if it's as hard as they say." Years later, I've found that it is, indeed, an excellent application deserving of obsession. I have also discovered that as you peel back the layers of BizTalk Server, it becomes a very intuitive product to use. This book will help you to do just that. We'll investigate BizTalk Server in manageable chunks, so that you're able to decipher and understand each of the individual puzzle pieces (or components) that, together, form the BizTalk Server 2006 product.

This book is written for those of you who have little or no knowledge of the product. You'll find that most of the examples in this book are relatively simple and can be completed in a fairly short amount of time. As the title implies, this book is geared toward providing a foundational base of knowledge of the application and its many components. The book is composed of 14 chapters, each building upon the lessons learned in the previous chapter:

- Chapter 1 introduces you to the product as a whole, with a brief discussion of the individual components.

- Chapter 2 covers XML technology for those readers who may not have had the opportunity to work with the markup language. XML is the backbone of BizTalk Server, and understanding it will pay dividends as you work through the chapter applications.

- Chapter 3 takes you through the BizTalk installation process. It's a friendlier process than you might expect, and you'll see why.

- Chapter 4 is a deeper look at BizTalk Server components and why and when you'll use them.

- Chapter 5 takes an overall look at the concept of messaging and its impact on BizTalk Server.

- Chapter 6 revisits XML technology with a deeper look at XML schemas and how they relate to messaging as a whole.

- Chapter 7 is a hands-on look at the BizTalk Mapper. You'll have an opportunity to transform messages from one format to another.

- Chapter 8 offers an exciting opportunity to work with BizTalk ports and locations. You'll take a look at the various methods for introducing messages into BizTalk Server.

- Chapter 9 continues the message routing discussion with BizTalk pipelines. You'll build an application that can slice and dice inbound messages, and deliver them to BizTalk Server in a manageable and consistent format.

- Chapter 10 introduces you to the all-powerful BizTalk orchestration. The orchestration is considered by many to be the powerhouse of the server product, and you'll have a chance to take one out for a spin.

- Chapter 11 covers some of the more advanced orchestration techniques, building on the lessons learned from the previous chapter.

- Chapter 12 addresses working with the business rules engine. We'll implement some dynamic logic enforcers that are called from within an orchestration.

- Chapter 13 discusses monitoring the activities taking place in your BizTalk Server implementation. You'll see how to use the tool commonly known as BAM (Business Activity Monitoring) to get an inside look at your data flow.

- Chapter 14 wraps things up with a discussion on deploying your BizTalk work out to the server itself.

After you have completed the individual lessons delivered through each of the chapters, I encourage you to follow up with *Pro BizTalk Server 2006* (available from Apress, http://www.apress.com) as your next step toward product mastery. It is my sincere hope that this book will help you toward that goal of mastery, and someday you'll look back on your integration career and find that this publication was the catalyst for starting something great.

Thank you so much for buying this book!

Daniel Woolston

CHAPTER 1

■■■

What Is BizTalk Server?

If you were to walk up to three developers and ask them to describe BizTalk Server, you would undoubtedly receive three different opinions. Here are some of the responses that I've received from a few of my peers:

"It's a messaging system for enterprise architecture."

"BizTalk allows you to connect different entities to one central location."

"It gives you a method of processing live messages."

"BTS lets me apply business rules to vendor data."

The amazing thing about these answers is that they're all correct. BizTalk Server 2006 is a collection of components that all seek to accomplish one task: integration.

In this chapter, we'll take a look at what BizTalk Server can do for an enterprise, and then have a quick tour of its components.

What Can BizTalk Do for You?

One of my previous consulting jobs in recent years was for a superstore retailer in Michigan. This particular corporation had seriously diverse enterprise architectures: data stored in Teradata, DB2, SQL Server 2000, and, believe it or not, some Access applications. All of these disparate systems were functional in their own realm, but integrating them proved to be quite challenging. The company's setup, shown in Figure 1-1, is not unlike that found in many organizations.

As you can see, this particular organization is a mess. How does something get this bad? Most companies tend to have two excuses:

- We built the various systems as we grew and had need.

- It's not broken, so there would be no financial gain from changing it to a more structured environment.

These are valid points. However, more and more, companies are beginning to find value in a service-oriented architecture (more of that in Chapter 4). Having the infrastructure geared toward rapid adaptation of vendor-supplied data and the ability to process that data within the rules of your own business logic has become a huge selling point for BizTalk Server. As enterprise architects begin to rethink their business processes, they become excited at what the product will enable them to do. They're able to connect a broader range of software to a central location, as shown in Figure 1-2.

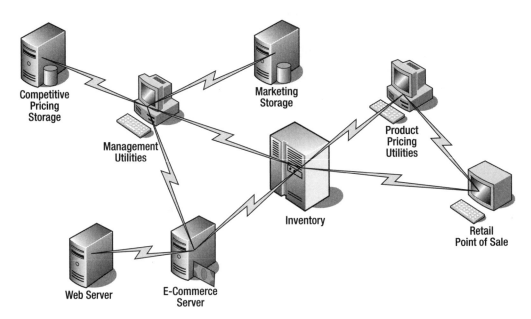

Figure 1-1. *An environment in need of structure*

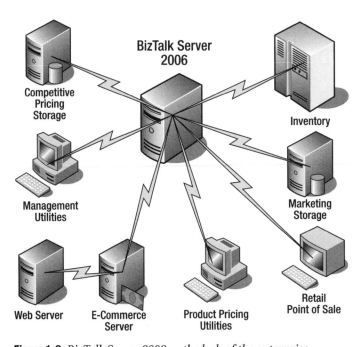

Figure 1-2. *BizTalk Server 2006 as the hub of the enterprise*

Integration through Adapters

With BizTalk, organizations are able to communicate with a variety of platforms and applications. How does that happen? I'm glad you asked.

Microsoft has created a set of default adapters that are your application-specific interfaces to the BizTalk messaging engine. And if Microsoft's adapters don't satisfy your needs, you may find the functionality available from one of the many third-party adapter vendors. Figure 1-3 illustrates how the server is able to communicate with a variety of protocols and applications by simply swapping out the interface adapter.

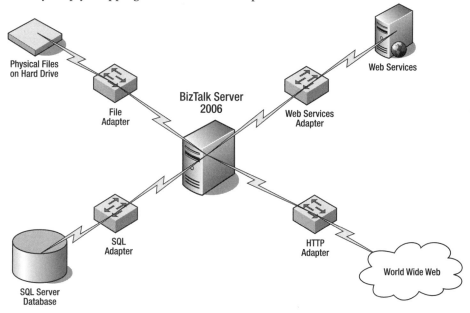

Figure 1-3. *A small sampling of the multilingual adapter world*

Figure 1-3 illustrates only four of the larger collection of adapters that Microsoft has provided for your integration needs. Table 1-1 lists commonly used Microsoft adapters.

Table 1-1. *BizTalk Server Adapters*

Adapter	Description
Web Services Adapter	Send and receive messages as SOAP packages over HTTP
File Adapter	Read and write files to the file system
MSMQ Adapter	Send and receive messages with Microsoft Message Queuing
HTTP Adapter	Send and receive messages via HTTP
WebSphere Adapter	Send and receive messages using WebSphere MQ by IBM
SMTP Adapter	Send messages via SMTP
POP3 Adapter	Receive e-mail messages and attachments
SharePoint Services Adapter	Access SharePoint document libraries
SQL Adapter	Interface with a SQL Server database

Microsoft has also been kind enough to provide some new corporate-software-specific adapters to help you integrate the application data into BizTalk. You'll find adapters for Siebel, PeopleSoft, and JD Edwards. As you begin to work with third-party application providers, you may find that the developers of the product will have a BizTalk Server 2006 adapter as part of the implementation package. And, of course, you're always welcome to build your own unique server adapter as well.

BizTalk Components

While the adapters are powerful components of the product, they are certainly not the only ones. As Figure 1-4 demonstrates, the BizTalk messaging engine is the main attraction of its surrounding tool set. Each of the applications built on top of the BizTalk messaging engine has a unique and powerful ability to either monitor or manipulate your data. Let's take a quick look at each of these applications.

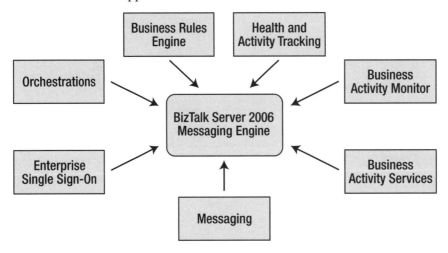

Figure 1-4. *BizTalk Server 2006 Applications*

Business Rules Engine

The rules engine allows you to apply business process logic against message data. Microsoft provides a full-featured tool for rules creation, called the Business Rule Composer, as shown in Figure 1-5. We'll visit this application in Chapter 12.

Orchestrations

The Orchestration Designer provides a unique graphical interface for routing, evaluating, and manipulating incoming and outgoing messages. Orchestrations also provide a means by which you can communicate with web services, databases, and other corporate entities. BizTalk Server can become the central player in a corporate service-oriented architecture, which (in my opinion) is the true selling point of the application as a whole. Figure 1-6 shows a sample orchestration that we'll build in Chapter 10, which discusses orchestrations in detail.

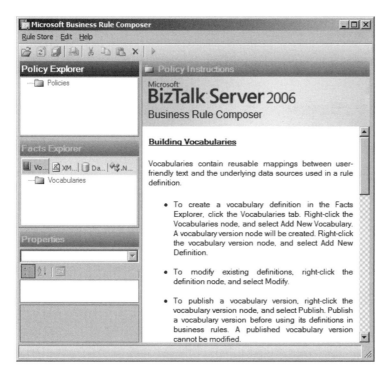

Figure 1-5. *The Business Rule Composer*

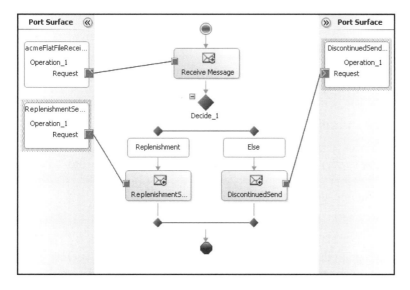

Figure 1-6. *A sample orchestration in the Orchestration Designer*

Health and Activity Tracking

Health and Activity Tracking (HAT), shown in Figure 1-7, is a helpful application for monitoring the BizTalk Messaging Engine and any corresponding orchestrations that you may be running against it.

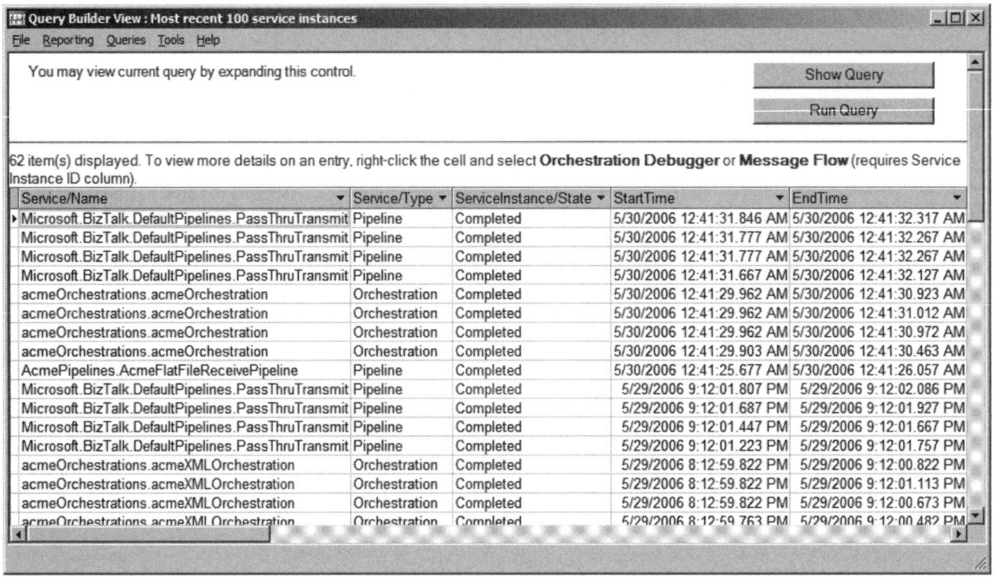

Figure 1-7. *Health and Activity Tracking utility*

Business Activity Monitoring

Business Activity Monitoring (BAM) gives nontechnical personnel a portal to view the data, in process, as shown in Figure 1-8. In Chapter 13, we'll visit the BAM portal.

Business Activity Services

BizTalk Business Activity Services feature set provides functionality for managing and instantiating integration relationships with various trading partners. It does that through an implementation of SharePoint Services that enables business users to interact with business processes as well as organizational trading partners.

Messaging

One could almost make the point that messaging is the core component of the BizTalk Server product. Messaging is not simply one particular application that you can start. It's a combination of adapters, pipelines, ports, and more that collaborate to effectively and efficiently manipulate and route your message data. In the following chapters, we'll examine the messaging concept with sample applications that will demonstrate the components' contributions to messaging as a whole.

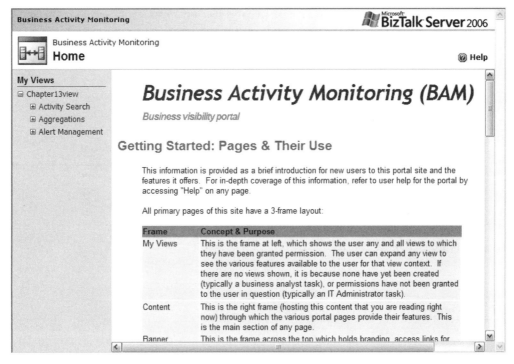

Figure 1-8. *Sample BAM portal*

Figure 1-9 illustrates a generic messaging flow. Don't get too hung up on the diagram just yet. As you progress through this book, it will all make sense.

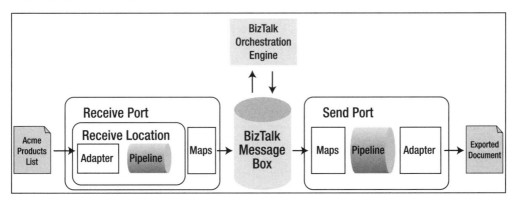

Figure 1-9. *Sample message flow*

Enterprise Single Sign-On

Enterprise Single Sign-On (SSO) is the process by which non-Windows authentication accounts can be granted or denied rights based on preferential mappings established by the

BizTalk administrator. This allows you to take in a message that has established authentication through the trading partner's own criteria and correspondingly map that authentication to an internal account within your enterprise. Figure 1-10 shows a generic SSO console interface.

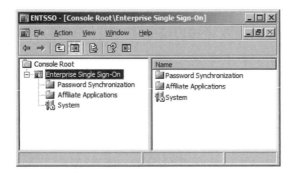

Figure 1-10. *Single Sign-On console*

Messages

As we are discussing the definition of BizTalk, we would be at a loss if we didn't discuss the one component that makes the whole thing tick: the message itself. Without incoming and outgoing messages, we wouldn't have any kind of data to process!

So what is a BizTalk message? Is there a difference between trading partner messages and the internal messages processed with the BizTalk engine?

In a general sense, a message is a file with inclusive data. For instance, the soda vendor for a particular retail store might send you a file with billable information for items delivered to your docks. That file could be anything from a comma-separated-values (CSV) text file to an HTML document delivered via the Internet. The method and the format are really inconsequential to BizTalk. All BizTalk really cares about is the data within those files. But there is a caveat to consuming that vendor's file.

In order for BizTalk Server to manipulate, route, or modify the incoming information, you must convert whatever document you're sent to XML. As you may have guessed, XML is the communication language of choice for the BizTalk messaging engine.

Information coming in needs to broken down, or *disassembled*, to the standardized XML format. As illustrated in Figure 1-11, an incoming CSV file, as supplied by the vendor, arrives via File Transfer Protocol (FTP) and is dropped into a file location on the network. The BizTalk adapter monitors that folder, and when it finds that a file has arrived, it sends the file off to the pipeline for reconstructive work that will morph it into the much-needed XML format. Once you have the vendor's data standardized, it's shipped off to the BizTalk messaging engine for processing.

As you can see, your incoming data will need a few modifications as it travels on the road to the BizTalk messaging engine. Fortunately, you have a few tools at your disposal that will make message transformation a lot easier. These include the Schema Editor, Pipeline Editor, and BizTalk Mapper.

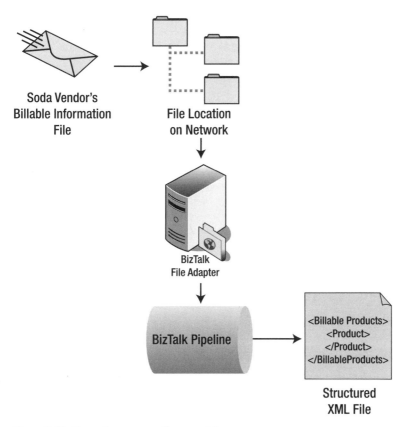

Figure 1-11. *Sample message disassembly*

Schema Editor

You'll use XML schemas quite liberally in your BizTalk development, and the Schema Editor provides an interface for quick and easy generation of those XML schemas, as shown in Figure 1-12. Don't worry if you're not sure exactly what an XML schema is. We'll be covering schemas in detail in Chapter 6. For now, you just need to know that a schema is an XML file that describes the structure of another XML file.

Pipeline Editor

To manipulate your message format on the way into the BizTalk engine, you can decode, disassemble, and otherwise parse the incoming format to meet the standard XML requirement. The Pipeline Editor provides a simple, graphical interface for converting the file, as shown in Figure 1-13.

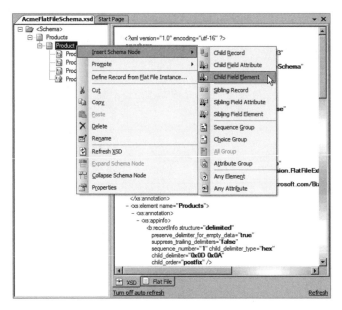

Figure 1-12. *BizTalk Schema Editor*

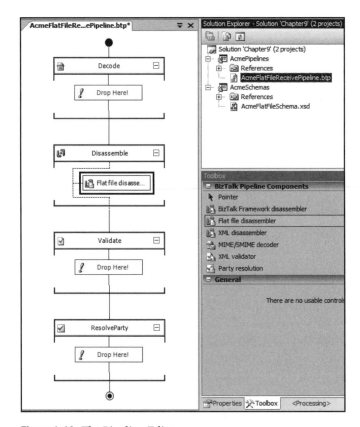

Figure 1-13. *The Pipeline Editor*

The BizTalk Mapper

So let's say that you have a generic billing XML format that your organization follows. Your soda vendor supplies you with a proprietary file that is nearly identical to yours, with the exception of a few columns of data. Wouldn't it be great if you could just parse the message to your XML format by simply mapping the incoming file format to the XML schema that your company prefers? Well, you're in luck, because the BizTalk Mapper does just that. As you can see in Figure 1-14, the Mapper is a drag-and-drop, matching game of sorts. You simply drag the relationships across the design board and match them to the corresponding fields.

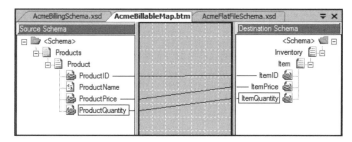

Figure 1-14. *The BizTalk Mapper*

There's quite a bit more functionality involved with the Mapper—so much, in fact, that Chapter 6 is dedicated to mapping messages.

Summary

Answering the question "What is BizTalk Server?" is a little more involved than simply saying that it's a "messaging, routing, business rules kind of product." It's a collection of like-minded tools that serve one purpose: integration.

The BizTalk product is huge. Unfortunately, many developers have this misconception that the immensity of BizTalk must indicate an associated degree of difficulty in learning the product. Learning to use BizTalk doesn't have to be difficult. If you take each of the individual tool sets separately and work with it (as you will during the course of the book), you'll find that this server application is not only powerful, but approachable and intuitive.

In Chapter 2, we will begin our journey by getting acquainted with the XML language. As XML is the force behind the product, you need to have a keen understanding of the syntax and usage of this standardized markup language. If you've worked with XML before, you can skim through the chapter and fill in any knowledge gaps that you find.

CHAPTER 2

■ ■ ■

Understanding XML

One of the things that I decided when I began outlining the contents for this book was that I wanted the book to be approachable by all developers, regardless of their exposure to BizTalk and its corresponding tool set. Because I truly desire to have you build "Foundation" skills with this guide, I believe that I should cover even the most basic details of the BizTalk product. And the most basic component for BizTalk Server 2006 is the XML message. XML is the language of choice for data going in and coming out of the BizTalk messaging engine.

To work fluently with BizTalk, you need to have a basic understanding of the XML language. I've read a plethora of .NET books that deal with XML syntax in some fashion, and typically, the authors seemed to take for granted that the reader has a full and comprehensive grip on the language. Unfortunately for those authors (and their readers as well), not everyone has had a chance to work with XML and build up that skill set. But I want to break that cycle. I want you to boldly jump into this book, without fear of the XML monster. And so we'll spend this chapter examining XML—its syntax and design. If you've worked with the language before, feel free to skim through these pages, making sure that you don't have any knowledge gaps before you proceed with the rest of the book.

The XML Language

When we speak of XML as a language, bear in mind that we use it in the context that XML is a vocabulary of *description*. Your initial perception may be that you would use the language as a method of communication, and that is partly true. XML is what is generally referred to as a *markup language*, in that it describes (or marks up) embedded or referenced data. We'll explore that concept in a moment, but first some context.

XML is relatively new in the technology timeline. It is the child of former markup languages, beginning with IBM's GML:

- *Generalized Markup Language (GML)* was developed in the late 1960s as a markup technology by IBM. It's generally accepted as the forefather of XML, wherein the concept of document structure is dictated by distinct structural elements.

- *Standard Generalized Markup Language (SGML)* built on the advances of GML and introduced a key innovation to the markup world: document structure validation. During the mid-1970s throughout the 1980s, SGML became quite popular as the document structure of choice for numerous industries. Most notably, the US Army required that all contractors submit their documentation in SGML format only. While the markup language is quite powerful, it is also extremely difficult to manipulate.

- *Extensible Markup Language (XML)* was the next step. As the Internet began to grow in popularity as well as complexity, it became apparent that HTML (also a child of SGML) was limited in document processing. A great need began to emerge, necessitating the introduction of a standardized methodology for describing structured data that was not only extensible, but also easy to implement. The answer came from XML in late 1996.

XML Structure

So now you know where XML came from. But what exactly does XML *do*? Well, as I said earlier, XML is a method of document description. For instance, let's suppose that my company has sent your company the following file:

```
wrench
13.85
101
1
3
socket
2.99
299
4
2
```

This information is virtually useless to your business processes without some form of description. This is where XML steps in to aid our communication. Add some descriptive elements to the file, and you'll find that the document is something that can be used intelligently:

```
<products>
  <product>
    <name>wrench</name>
    <price>13.85</price>
    <id>101</id>
    <quantityonhand>1</quantityonhand>
    <quantityonorder>3</quantityonorder>
  </product>
  <product>
    <name>socket</name>
    <price>2.99</price>
    <id>299</id>
    <quantityonhand>4</quantityonhand>
    <quantityonorder>2</quantityonorder>
  </product>
</products>
```

Even without an in-depth knowledge of XML coding, you can get a feel for what the document is trying to convey in terms of content and structure. And that leads to the next logical step in our discussion: basic syntax.

Basic XML Syntax

When we talk about basic syntax, we're really referring to the simple rules that you should follow to maintain a well-formed XML file. Most companies that accept XML messages will turn away malformed documents, and so a strict adherence to the rules becomes essential when dealing with XML structure.

The core concept of XML is that all messages are built with elements. As you can see in the previous XML example, it includes descriptive "tags" that suggest the purpose of the data within its boundaries: `<products>`, `<product>`, `<name>`, `<price>`, and so on. We refer to these tags as *elements*. Our list of syntax requirements begins with a rule about including elements.

Elements Must Open and Close

When you open an element by declaring `<product>`, you'll need to have a corresponding closing element. The closing element simply prefixes the element name with a slash: `</product>`.

The opening and closing elements will surround the embedded data, like this:

```
<name>wrench</name>
```

This example declares an element that will hold data for a field called `name`. The embedded data, `wrench`, is attributed to the element `name`.

So what if you have an element with no data, which is quite possible with data processing? Instead of using `<product></product>`, you could choose to use a single element: `<product />`. You add the slash to the tail end of the opening element, and it will consequently close that element, indicating to any outside processing that this particular piece is empty.

Elements Should Nest Correctly

If you've worked with `If/Then` statements, you understand the importance of proper nesting. XML is no different. You'll need to maintain correct element placement, as in this example:

```
<product>
    <name>wrench</name>
    <price>13.85</price>
    <id>101</id>
    <quantityonhand>1</quantityonhand>
    <quantityonorder>3</quantityonorder>
</product>
```

The following is *incorrect* placement:

```
<product>
    <name>wrench</name>
    <price>13.85</price>
    <id>101</id>
    <quantityonhand>1
    <quantityonorder>3
    </quantityonhand>
    </quantityonorder>
</product>
```

In the incorrect version, the `</quantityonhand>` element is not closed correctly. This will cause any validation on the XML file to fail miserably.

Declare the File As XML

As you build your own XML files, you'll need to declare that the file is indeed an XML file. Otherwise, there would be little distinction to a client application that this is XML and not just some text-based flat file of generic formatting. You do that by including an XML declaration at the start of the document:

```
<?xml version="1.0" encoding="ISO-8859-1"?>
<products>
  <product>
    <name>wrench</name>
    <price>13.85</price>
    <id>101</id>
    <quantityonhand>1</quantityonhand>
    <quantityonorder>3</quantityonorder>
  </product>
  <product>
    <name>socket</name>
    <price>2.99</price>
    <id>299</id>
    <quantityonhand>4</quantityonhand>
    <quantityonorder>2</quantityonorder>
  </product>
</products>
```

The first line indicates that the XML file will be using the 1.0 XML standard (according to the Word Wide Web Consortium, `http://www.w3.org`) and will use the ISO-8859-1 character set for the notation text.

When this document passes into a parsing process, it will have made the proclamation to the handling application that it is an XML file and should be handled as such.

Include a Root Element

Another requisite to the XML syntax is the inclusion of at least a single, root element that encapsulates the nested elements within. In our sample XML file, the `<products>` element is set as the root. As you begin to work with the XML editor in BizTalk, you'll also notice that BizTalk will, by default, declare a root node for you.

XML Attributes

If you've worked with HTML, you'll feel right at home with XML attributes:

```
<img src="http://www.danwoolston.com/portals/0/msftday5a.jpg" />
```

The `src` within the opening element indicates that this image element will find its associated object at the included web address, or source (`src`), as shown. We call these element descriptors *attributes*. You'll see them a lot with BizTalk XML files, and so it is essential that you understand their usefulness.

In general, an attribute is used to describe an overall fact of the element and its nested elements that are buried within the tag. For instance, let's say you have a car element:

```
<car>
  <price>14500</price>
</car>
```

If you wanted to add manufacturer data, you could easily add a corresponding manufacturer tag:

```
<car>
  <manufacturer>Buick</manufacturer>
  <price>14500</price>
</car>
```

However, because the manufacturer is really associated with the car as a whole, many prefer to declare it as an attribute by adding it to the opening, parent element:

```
<car manufacturer="Buick" >
  <price>14500</price>
</car>
```

Attributes must also be enclosed within quotes as shown, if you want to maintain a well-formed document structure. As you can see, it's a little more organized. As you progress farther with BizTalk and XML, you'll find yourself using attributes quite liberally.

XML Validation

Creating an XML file is not really all that difficult. However, creating a file that meets the requirements of a vendor may prove to be a bit harder. An organization may have a set structure for the XML it will accept, and consequently will validate that the file you send meets those constraints.

The basic premise of XML validation is that messages of a specified type must also adhere to a specified structure. If they follow the rules and are well formed, they pass validation. For instance, let's suppose that you are submitting a product order to a business-to-business (B2B) retailer. You have this file:

```
<?xml version="1.0" encoding="ISO-8859-1"?>
<products>
  <product>
    <name>wrench</name>
    <price>13.85</price>
    <id>101</id>
    <quantityonhand>1</quantityonhand>
    <quantityonorder>3</quantityonorder>
  </product>
```

```
<product>
  <name>socket</name>
  <price>2.99</price>
  <id>299</id>
  <quantityonhand>4</quantityonhand>
  <quantityonorder>2</quantityonorder>
</product>
</products>
```

If we eliminate the data and redundant <product> elements, we're left with the following basic structure:

```
<?xml version="1.0" encoding="ISO-8859-1"?>
<products>
  <product>
    <name></name>
    <price></price>
    <id></id>
    <quantityonhand></quantityonhand>
    <quantityonorder></quantityonorder>
  </product>
</products>
```

But what if your trading partner has the following format?

```
<?xml version="1.0" encoding="ISO-8859-1"?>
<products>
  <product>
    <name></name>
    <price></price>
    <id></id>
    <quantityrequested></quantityrequested>
  </product>
</products>
```

Obviously, your current format would fail when validated by the retailer. So how can you obtain the proper structure and validate against that preferred structure? The answer can be found with XML schemas.

XML Schemas

A schema file is an XML file that describes how an associated data file should be structured. The schema file is void of content data, and rightly so. Its sole purpose is to dictate how the linked XML file should be constructed.

A Sample Schema

Before we proceed with the specifics of schemas, let's take a look at a schema that I've generated with BizTalk's Schema Editor. I'll use the trading partners format shown in the preceding example as the basis for the file.

```
<?xml version="1.0" encoding="utf-16" ?>
<xs:schema xmlns:b="http://schemas.microsoft.com/BizTalk/2003"
  xmlns="http://AcmeSchemas.ProductsSchema"
  targetNamespace="http://AcmeSchemas.ProductsSchema"
  xmlns:xs="http://www.w3.org/2001/XMLSchema">
<xs:element name="Products">
  <xs:complexType>
    <xs:sequence>
      <xs:element name="Product">
        <xs:complexType>
          <xs:sequence>
            <xs:element name="Name" type="xs:string" />
            <xs:element name="Price" type="xs:decimal" />
            <xs:element name="id" type="xs:int" />
            <xs:element name="quantityrequested" type="xs:int" />
          </xs:sequence>
        </xs:complexType>
      </xs:element>
    </xs:sequence>
  </xs:complexType>
</xs:element>
</xs:schema>
```

Don't be shocked by the complexity of the file. As you read about the various XML elements, you'll begin to get a feel for what BizTalk has generated here.

So what does this file do for us? It provides a means of validating incoming XML files to ensure that they maintain the same consistency of structure that we expect to use in our business processes. So how do we use this to validate the data file? In BizTalk, we'll use the schema file as a key component for screening data files that are being fed to the system. We'll also be using the file as a source for creating new messages and passing them around the messaging engine in the BizTalk environment. Figure 2-1 illustrates the basic traffic pattern of XML validation.

So you know why we'll be using schemas. Now let's concentrate on the various schema elements and their meanings.

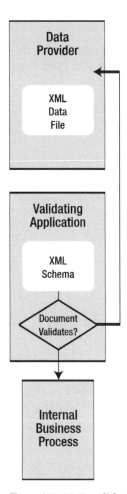

Figure 2-1. *XML validation path*

XML Schema Structure

Because a schema file is also an XML file, it's prefaced with the appropriate XML declaration:

```
<?xml version="1.0" encoding="utf-16" ?>
```

All of the normal, well-formed rules still apply to schemas, so you need to keep the afore-mentioned rules in mind when creating or troubleshooting schemas.

The root element will come in the form of the schema declaration. In much the same fashion that you declare the document to be an XML file, you also declare the contents to be schema-based elements:

```
<xs:schema xmlns:b="http://schemas.microsoft.com/BizTalk/2003"
  xmlns="http://AcmeSchemas.ProductsSchema"
  targetNamespace="http://AcmeSchemas.ProductsSchema"
  xmlns:xs="http://www.w3.org/2001/XMLSchema">
```

When you start working with the BizTalk Schema Editor, you'll get a better feel for the namespaces that are included within the schema declaration. For now, be aware that `<xs:schema>` is the primary element that you'll need for the file to be recognized as a proper schema.

Next, let's look at the actual structure of the schema and how it relates to the XML data file.

```
<xs:element name="Products">
  <xs:complexType>
    <xs:sequence>
      <xs:element name="Product">
        <xs:complexType>
          <xs:sequence>
            <xs:element name="Name" type="xs:string" />
            <xs:element name="Price" type="xs:decimal" />
            <xs:element name="id" type="xs:int" />
            <xs:element name="quantityrequested" type="xs:int" />
          </xs:sequence>
        </xs:complexType>
      </xs:element>
    </xs:sequence>
  </xs:complexType>
</xs:element>
</xs:schema>
```

Translated to plain English, this reads as follows:

We expect that the incoming file will have a root element with a name of Products. That Products element will be made up of one or more Product elements. Each individual Product element will have four individual nested elements that will appear in the following order: Name, Price, id, and quantityrequested. Also, each of the nested elements will adhere to the proper data types as shown (string, decimal, integer, and integer).

Before we move on, let's go over a few things about the various schema elements in the sample schema.

<xs:complexType>

Elements in a schema file will generally fall into one of two type categories:

- *Complex types* can have nested elements as well as attributes.

- *Simple types* cannot have nested elements or attributes for the current element.

A majority of the work that we'll do with schemas will ultimately involve complex types. Because our `<products>` element will have one to many `<product>` elements submitted, we add the complexType and include the nested elements within.

<xs:sequence>

When we throw in a schema sequence, we're asking that the elements to follow need to be sent in the same order as shown in the schema. In our sample schema, we have a series of elements that the data file will submit:

```
<xs:sequence>
  <xs:element name="Name" type="xs:string" />
  <xs:element name="Price" type="xs:decimal" />
  <xs:element name="id" type="xs:int" />
  <xs:element name="quantityrequested" type="xs:int" />
</xs:sequence>
```

For our sample data file to validate correctly, we'll need to submit the elements in the proper order as dictated by the sequence:

```
<?xml version="1.0" encoding="ISO-8859-1"?>
<products>
  <product>
    <name>wrench</name>
    <price>13.85</price>
    <id>101</id>
    <quantityrequested>4</quantityrequested>
  </product>
  <product>
    <name>socket</name>
    <price>2.99</price>
    <id>299</id>
    <quantityrequested>2</quantityrequested>
  </product>
</products>
```

If for some reason our elements were out of order:

```
<product>
  <name>wrench</name>
  <id>101</id>
  <price>13.85</price>
  <quantityrequested>4</quantityrequested>
</product>
```

the validation process would fail for this particular document.

<xs: element type>

One of the cool things about schemas is that we can require that any incoming data be of specific types. We can ask that prices be supplied in decimal format. We can ask that quantities be integers. There are a multitude of schema types. The following are the more frequently used types:

- xs:boolean

- xs:byte

- xs:date

- xs:dateTime

- xs:decimal

- xs:double

- xs:float

- xs:int

- xs:integer

- xs:short

- xs:string

- xs:time

As you progress through the book, you'll find yourself relying on data types more often as you seek to apply constraints to the data. For example, it would be a bad thing to attempt multiplication against a string. Establishing data types helps to avoid that error. You simply assign them as attributes to the appropriate element and let the validator do the rest:

```
<xs:element name="Price" type="xs:decimal" />
```

Summary

We've taken a cursory look at XML and XML schemas, so that as you work through the book, the syntax of the message that you'll be working with won't seem so foreign. I encourage you to seek out an in-depth publication on XML. The more you know about this markup language, the better served you will be in your messaging endeavors.

In the next chapter, we'll finally begin working with BizTalk Server 2006! We'll take a walk through an initial installation of the product. I think you'll be pleasantly surprised at how quick and easy it is, particularly compared with the installation process for previous versions of the product.

■■■

CHAPTER 3

BizTalk Server 2006 Installation

My first experience with the BizTalk product was installing BizTalk Server 2004 on a single PC. One would think that such an installation would be a quick and easy process. One would be wrong. My initial attempt at getting BizTalk 2004 up and running was an *extremely* frustrating endeavor. On my final, and ultimately, successful try, I was able to get the BizTalk service up and running and actually pass messages—at 3:00 in the morning! Many of the developers that I've spoken with unanimously agree that installing the 2004 version was not a pleasant experience. Between the massive amount of prerequisites and the ongoing configuration problems, it was nothing short of miraculous if you actually got the product installed and running on the first try. So it is with much excitement that I announce that one of the prominent features of the 2006 release of the product is the streamlined installation process. What, at one time, took a good portion of a day (or days) to install and configure, now takes a few hours. In this chapter, you will do just that.

Because many of you will be using the product with Windows XP or Windows Server 2003, I'll cover the end-to-end process for those two operating systems. Note that the installation that you are performing in this chapter is for the purposes of testing the application as you progress through the rest of the book. You will not be configuring SharePoint Services (which are not available on Windows XP) during this installation, which will help you get up and running a bit faster.

Windows XP–Specific Issues

Before we get started with the installation process, we should first take a look at some of the issues related to running BizTalk on an XP box.

Partition format: You need to have Windows XP installed on an NTFS formatted drive, not a FAT32 drive. You'll need to convert the drive to NTFS by running `convert c: /fs:ntfs` (if you're converting the C: drive) in a Command Prompt window, as shown in Figure 3-1.

Figure 3-1. *Converting to NTFS*

■**Caution** Converting a drive does carry with it a minor amount of risk. You should take appropriate backup measures if you have anything critical on your PC.

Computer name: Your PC's computer name must be 15 characters or fewer; otherwise, you will be unable to configure BizTalk Server, and that would be bad. If necessary, shorten the computer name and reboot.

SharePoint Services: The Microsoft SharePoint Services Adapter and Business Activity Services (BAS) functionality of BizTalk Server will be unavailable on a Windows XP installation. It's not possible to run SharePoint Services on an XP box, as shown in Figure 3-2.

Figure 3-2. *SharePoint Services is a no-go on an XP box.*

Installing BizTalk Software Prerequisites

A common misconception is that BizTalk Server 2006 is a stand-alone product. I've talked with a few developers who were under the assumption that they could simply drop the disc in and go from there. It's a bit of a shock to some when they find out how many other Microsoft products need to be on the box before you can even think about installing the server. We'll take a look at those products and their installation, and then move on to BizTalk installation after you have your computer ready.

You should install the following products prior to adding BizTalk to the PC:

- Internet Information Services (IIS) 5.1 (Windows XP) or 6.0 (Windows 2003)

- .NET Framework 1.1 (SQL Server 2000) or 2.0 (SQL Server 2005, installed by default)

- Microsoft Excel 2003 with Service Pack (SP) 2

- Microsoft Visual Studio 2005

- SQL Server 2005 (recommended) or SQL Server 2000 with SP4

I'm going to assume that you have the operating system installed already. I do want to remind you that if you're on an XP box, you'll need the operating system bumped up to SP2. If you're installing on Windows 2003 Server, you'll need to patch your server with SP1. Service packs are available from the Microsoft Downloads website (http://www.microsoft.com/downloads).

■Note If you're installing BizTalk on a production box, you most likely will not need the development products (Visual Studio, Office applications, and so on). Depending on the options that you choose for the production environment, you'll want to check the particular dependencies of the individual BizTalk components.

Internet Information Service (IIS)

BizTalk will use IIS for a lot of things, most notably HTTP and SOAP Adapters, and SSL encryption.

Installing IIS 5.1 on Windows XP

On Windows XP, install IIS 5.1 as follows:

1. Open the Control Panel.

2. Click Add or Remove Programs, and then Add/Remove Windows Components.

3. Find Internet Information Services and check it.

4. Click Finish to exit the wizard.

Installing IIS 6.0 on Windows Server 2003

To install IIS on your Windows Server 2003, you'll need to first enable the application server components:

1. Click Start ➤ All Programs ➤ Administrative Tools ➤ Manage Your Server.

2. In the first window, click Add a Role.

3. A preliminary steps window will pop up. Review the information, and then click Next.

4. The Configure Your Server Wizard starts. Highlight Application Server in the list of server roles.

5. The Application Server Options dialog box appears. Make sure that Enable ASP.NET is checked, as shown in Figure 3-3. Then click Next to continue.

6. Review the list in the Summary of Selections dialog box to ensure that it reflects your intentions, and then click Next to continue.

7. Windows will now configure the server to include IIS functionality. You will most likely be prompted for your Windows 2003 installation CD. Drop the disc in and click OK to continue. After a moment, the installation will continue to completion.

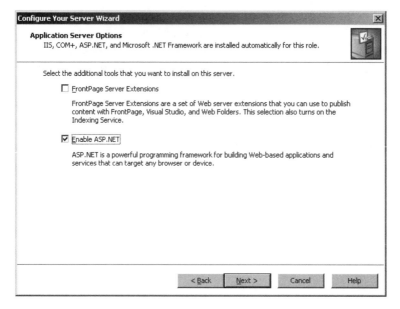

Figure 3-3. *Selecting ASP.NET configuration*

.NET Framework

If you're using SQL Server 2005, which I recommend, .NET Framework 2.0 will be installed with Visual Studio 2005.

If you are using SQL Server 2000 and Business Activity Monitoring (BAM) alerts, you'll need .NET Framework 1.1 installed. Download the .NET Framework from here:

```
http://go.microsoft.com/fwlink/?LinkId=55146
```

SP1.1 is available from this site:

```
http://go.microsoft.com/fwlink/?LinkId=62529
```

Security Update 1.1 is available here:

```
http://go.microsoft.com/fwlink/?LinkId=62531
```

You will probably need to reboot after installing the .NET Framework.

Microsoft Excel

Microsoft Excel is needed to run BAM. I would highly recommend installing it if you want to take advantage of all of the functionality offered by BizTalk Server 2006. Follow these steps to install Excel 2003:

1. Insert your Microsoft Office 2003 installation disc and wait for autorun to start the installation program.

2. Enter your 25-character product key in the Product Key dialog box, and then click Next.

3. Enter your user name, initials, and organization in the User Information dialog box, and then click Next.

4. Accept the End User License Agreement (EULA) and click Next.

5. Select Custom Install in the Type of Installation dialog box, and then click Next.

6. When you get to the Custom Setup dialog box, select Excel, and then click Next to continue.

7. Click Install.

When the installation completes, you'll want to grab the service pack from here:

`http://go.microsoft.com/fwlink/?LinkId=55034`

Microsoft Visual Studio

You'll definitely want to install Visual Studio 2005. It will become your primary development environment for all things BizTalk. At the bare minimum, you'll need to install at least the C# components of the product, but I recommend also installing the VB.NET component, as you may be using it for other work on the same box.

1. Insert the Visual Studio 2005 installation disc.

2. Click Install Visual Studio 2005, and then click Next.

3. Enter your appropriate product key on the agreement form and click Next. You'll notice that the installation program is notifying you of the various components that must be installed prior to installing Visual Studio 2005. Fortunately, it will handle that internally.

4. In the Select Features to Install dialog box, remove all but C# and VB.NET. Then click Install.

5. You'll most likely be prompted to reboot during installation. After booting, the installation will continue.

6. When all is said and done, click Finish to exit the installation process.

Microsoft SQL Server

Microsoft SQL Server is a core component for BizTalk. Many of the data processes will store and retrieve operational data there. You can use SQL Server 2000 with the product, but I recommend using SQL Server 2005 if at all possible.

Installing SQL Server 2005

Follow these steps to install SQL Server 2005:

1. Insert the SQL Server 2005 disc.

2. Accept the agreement in the End User License Agreement dialog box, and then click Next.

3. Click Next to continue through the Installing Prerequisites dialog box.

4. Click Next to continue through the Welcome dialog box.

5. Click Next after passing the prerequisites check in the System Requirements dialog box.

6. Fill in the Registration Information form, and then click Next.

7. You'll now be asked what components you would like to install. Select components, and then click Next. As shown in Figure 3-4, I recommend choosing the following, to allow you to work with the entire BizTalk product:

- SQL Server Database Services

- Analysis Services

- Reporting Services

- Notification Services

- Integration Services

- Workstation Components

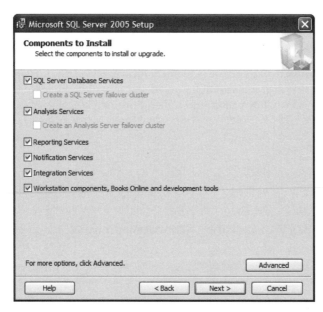

Figure 3-4. *Selecting the tools*

8. Select Default Instance in the Instance Name dialog box, and then click Next.

9. In the Service Account dialog box, make sure Customize for Each Service Account is unchecked. Select Use the Built-In System Account for authentication, as shown in Figure 3-5. Then click Next.

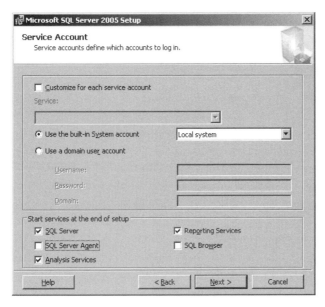

Figure 3-5. *Selecting authentication for SQL Server*

10. In the next dialog box, select Windows Authentication Mode, and then click Next.

11. Accept the default settings in the Collation Settings dialog box and click Next.

12. Accept the defaults in the Error and Usage Report Settings dialog box and click Next.

13. Click Install and take a break. It might take a few minutes to complete.

14. Reboot the computer when the installation has finished.

Configuring SQL Server 2005

Before moving on, you should do a bit of SQL Server configuration. Microsoft recommends that you disable the Shared Memory protocol on SQL Server 2005. Under certain stress conditions, your server could degrade in performance with this protocol enabled on the same box that BizTalk Server 2006 is running in parallel.

1. Click Start ➤ All Programs ➤ Microsoft SQL Server 2005 ➤ Configuration Tools ➤ SQL Server Configuration Manager.

2. Expand the Network Configuration node, and then click on the Protocols Node to bring up the appropriate entries in the right pane, as shown in Figure 3-6.

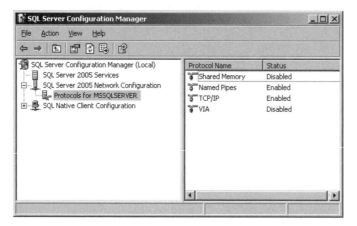

Figure 3-6. *Disabling the Shared Memory protocol*

3. Right-click the Shared Memory entry and select Disable.

4. Close the configuration tool and reboot the computer.

With all the prerequisites installed, you're now ready for action! Which brings us to the main event: BizTalk Server 2006.

Installing and Configuring BizTalk Server 2006

As I said at the start of the chapter, installing the actual server component is relatively simple compared with installing the previous version. One of the biggest improvements to the installation process is the inclusion of prerequisite files within an accessible .cab file that can be easily downloaded from the Web.

Installing BizTalk

Before you take off on a clicking frenzy, make sure that you've successfully installed all of the prerequisite software and have closed any open software. Then follow these steps:

1. Drop your disc into the drive and select the Install option when prompted.

2. In the Customer Information form, enter the appropriate information, and then click Next to continue.

3. Accept the Licensing Agreement and click Next to continue.

4. Accept the default selections in the Component Installation dialog box, and then click Next to continue.

■**Note** If you're installing on Windows XP, you'll notice that Business Activity Services (BAS) is grayed out in the Component Installation list. That's because Windows XP can't run SharePoint Services, so the prerequisite installation invalidates this tool.

---

5. In the next dialog box, you'll be asked how you would like to deal with the missing pre-requisite files (not applications). You're welcome to download the .cab file and use it in place, but I generally just select the downloadable option. Click Next to continue after you have made your selection.

6. You'll see the Summary dialog box, showing the components that will be installed, as shown in Figure 3-7. (As my installation is on a new XP box, the list is lengthy.) Click Install to begin the installation process. Be aware that the install program will want to reboot, but the process will resume on its own.

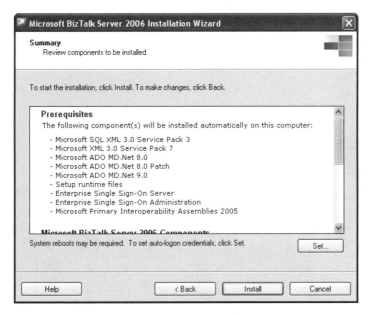

Figure 3-7. *Beginning the download process*

7. After the updates have been applied, the Server component will automatically install with everything else. Finally, you'll be greeted by the completion dialog box. You'll need to configure the server, so leave the Launch Configuration option checked and click Finish.

Configuring BizTalk Server on Windows XP

Because, for the purposes of this book, you are configuring BizTalk on a single PC server installation, you'll be using the Basic Configuration setting. Before you configure the server, note the following:

- You should empty the event log prior to configuration, as a full log will hinder the configuration.

- The account you've used to log on to the server (Windows XP box) must be a member of the local admin group and must also have system admin rights on the SQL Server installation.

Follow these steps to configure the server:

1. In the Configuration window, select Basic Configuration, as shown in Figure 3-8.

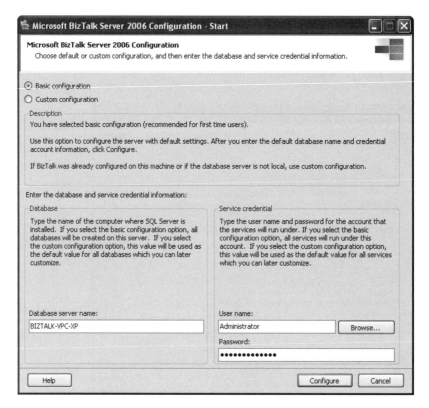

Figure 3-8. *Configuring the server*

2. Make sure that the database name is listed properly for the SQL Server installation that you completed earlier.

3. Use the Browse button to find the administrative account that you wish to use. Click Configure when complete.

4. BizTalk will kindly inform you of what it is about to update and notify you of any inconsistencies by adding an exclamation point to anything that may have configuration issues. Clicking Next will move you on your way.

When all is said and done, the server will be installed, configured, and ready for action!

Summary

If you've had the pleasure (read sarcasm here) of installing BizTalk Server 2004, then you'll surely appreciate the new 2006 installation process. I seriously dreaded the thought of having to install BizTalk Server 2004 on a fresh install of Windows because of the millions of patches and reboots that had to be done before I could even attempt to install BizTalk. Microsoft has made tremendous progress with the new install package, and I find that I don't dread installing the product so much.

I want to, once again, remind you that this installation process is particular and stream-lined for the book's purposes of testing the application. I do encourage you to visit Microsoft's BizTalk site for the full up-to-date installation information, at http://www.microsoft.com/biztalk.

If you're installing BizTalk Server in a production environment, you'll want to spend more time with Microsoft's documentation on the subject. You can find the current recommendations at this URL:

http://www.microsoft.com/biztalk/techinfo/whitepapers/default.mspx

Because we will not be using BAS in this book, you did not install and configure Share-Point Services. If you would like to investigate BAS after you have a good grounding in BizTalk skills, I encourage you to follow up this book with *Pro BizTalk Server 2006* (Apress, ISBN: 1-59059-699-4).

CHAPTER 4

■ ■ ■ ■

BizTalk Server 2006 Components

Now that you've installed the product, it would really be in your best interest to understand exactly what you've placed on your machine. Various applications have suddenly appeared in your programs list, and a multitude of database changes have occurred. In this chapter, we'll take a look at the server applications that you've gained as a result of our installation, as well as the database entities.

A Quick Tour of BizTalk Components

When you installed BizTalk Server 2006 (in Chapter 3), you also installed a variety of components that each serves a unique and practical purpose:

- BizTalk Server 2006 Administration Console

- BizTalk Server 2006 Configuration

- BizTalk Server 2006 Documentation

- Business Activity Monitoring

- BizTalk Web Services Publishing Wizard

- Microsoft Business Rule Composer

- Rules Engine Deployment Wizard

- Health and Activity Tracking

- Tracking Profile Editor

These applications are available through the BizTalk programs group (Start ➤ All Programs ➤ Microsoft BizTalk Server 2006).

■Note Obviously, with your particular installation, you may have a different set of components, depending on the options selected when you first installed the product.

In this section, we'll take a cursory look at each of the applications. During the course of this book, you will interact with most of them. After you've had the opportunity to work with these applications, you'll find (in hindsight) that they really were not as difficult to use as you may have perceived. Many assume that BizTalk is an incredibly hard technology with a steep learning curve. I'm confident that as you work through the examples in this book, you'll find that the applications tend to be very intuitive and somewhat self-describing.

BizTalk Server 2006 Administration Console

I refer to the BizTalk Server Administration Console application as the "hub" of the product line. It is the center point of all activity, and you'll find yourself using it quite a bit. One of the coolest features of the application is that the main page has a series of easy-access links that drive other content. If you're looking for online help or communities, you'll be able to arrive there from here. Figure 4-1 gives you an idea of the functionality available through the Administration Console.

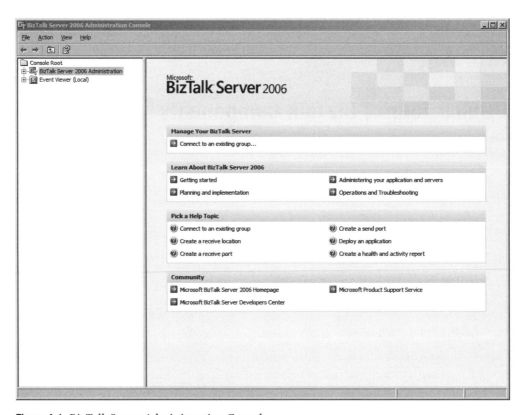

Figure 4-1. *BizTalk Server Administration Console*

One of the first links that you should click is Getting Started. You'll notice that BizTalk inquires as to whether you would prefer the online or local version of help. I prefer to use the web help, as it is more up-to-date. If, however, you lack connectivity on this box, you'll want to select the local version. After you've worked through this book, I encourage you to revisit the help page to continue your education through the tutorials and common developer tasks.

In the left panel of the Administration Console, notice that a few nodes are listed in the tree view. Expand both of the nodes fully, as shown in Figure 4-2.

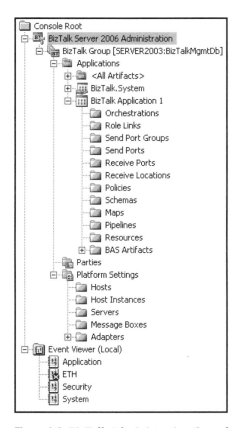

Figure 4-2. *BizTalk Administration Console nodes*

If you've ever had a chance to work with BizTalk 2004, one of the first things that you'll notice about the BizTalk 2006 Administration Console is that it is now an application-based model. Rather than just throwing all ports, orchestrations, pipelines, and other components into one big pool, you're now able to stage your work around the concept that the BizTalk application is the centerpiece of activity.

In much the same way that you would deploy an ASP.NET web application to IIS, you can deploy a BizTalk application to the server. A default application (BizTalk Application 1) has already been created for you. As you scan down the list of components, you'll see that you have a folder for each of the application pieces. With earlier versions, you would have to use goofy and complex naming conventions if you wanted to organize your integration tools. Having the ability to think in terms of an application helps to make sense of it all. Note that the application view exists only in the BizTalk Administration Console; it's not available within Visual Studio.

Also notice that you have easy access to the Event Viewer from within the Administration Console. As you troubleshoot your broken processes, you'll find yourself stopping here first.

You will become quite familiar with the Administration Console, as you will use it frequently throughout this book.

BizTalk Server Configuration

In the previous chapter, you actually skipped most of the BizTalk Server 2006 Configuration application, because you opted for the basic configuration. We're not going to reconfigure the server at this point, but I do want to cover it in brief, so that when you do need to make configuration changes, you'll know where to go.

When you open the Configuration application, you should see a window like the one shown in Figure 4-3.

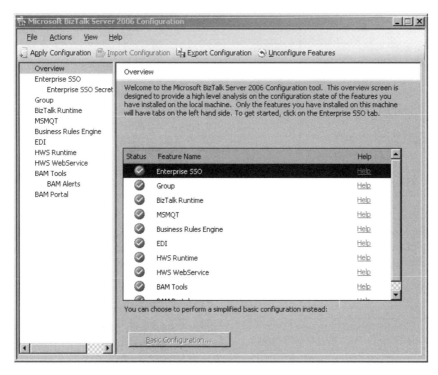

Figure 4-3. *The Configuration application*

The primary purpose of the Configuration tool is to allow you to modify a majority of the application user accounts. If you want to modify the current configuration, you'll need to click the Unconfigure Features button on the toolbar and select the particular section that you wish to modify, as shown in Figure 4-4.

One thing that you should do before continuing with the book is to export your current configuration. Clicking the Export Configuration button will kick off the process. Doing this will export the configuration settings to an XML file (see Figure 4-5) that you can use if you ever need to reinstall the server application. A simple import of the saved configuration will allow you to get back up and running in no time at all.

■**Caution** Use care when configuring your server, because bad things can happen when it's configured improperly. If a particular component fails to configure, this will be reported by the Configuration tool.

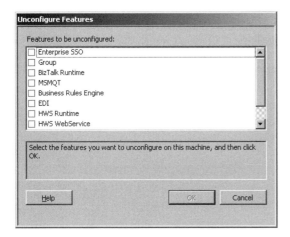

Figure 4-4. *Unconfiguring BizTalk features*

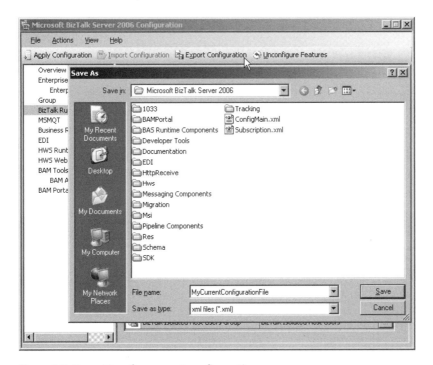

Figure 4-5. *Exporting the current configuration*

BizTalk Server Documentation

Documentation is a pretty self-explanatory option. I encourage you to check in with the documentation after you've finished with this book to fill in any knowledge gaps that you may have concerning the product. Definitely take a look at the Getting Started and BizTalk Server 2006 Tutorials sections, as they are invaluable to your progress with the product.

BAM Portal Web Site

Perhaps one of the most misunderstood components of BizTalk Server is Business Activity Monitoring (BAM). I've asked a few people what they thought BAM provided, and I don't think that I received the same answer twice. We will cover BAM in detail in Chapter 13, but for now, you should be aware that you have access to the BAM site, which was generated for you during the installation, as shown in Figure 4-6. Despite the page's appearance, it is *not* a SharePoint site and will not be managed as such. If you've opted to install the portal, you'll find the link for it in the same Start menu programs group as the main application.

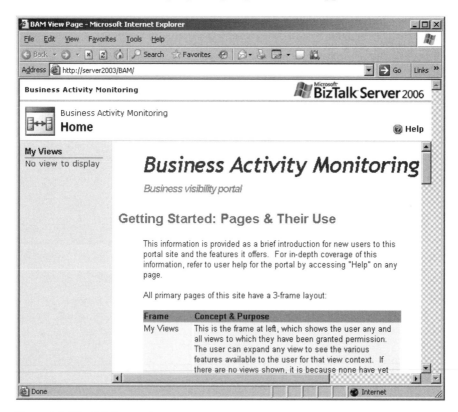

Figure 4-6. *The BAM portal page*

In brief, BAM allows you to monitor the in-process activity on your server. What's really cool about the technology is that it enables nontechnical business users to have an inward look at what exactly is going on in their integration enterprise. So if you have 500 crates of product sitting in a warehouse, waiting for approval (a BizTalk process), a top-level executive can take note of that and make the appropriate calls to expedite the path to approval. This is a huge selling point for IT directors looking to convince their bosses that BizTalk is the right fit for their company.

■**Note** BAM does not give you visibility into the health and well-being of the BizTalk Server. You need to implement Microsoft Operations Manager (http://www.microsoft.com/mom/default.mspx) for full health and process monitoring.

BizTalk Web Services Publishing Wizard

In the ever-growing service-oriented architecture push, we find that BizTalk has grasped that trend with its ability to host portions of its structure on the Internet as a web service. Notably, orchestrations and schemas can now be made available directly from the Web, as illustrated in Figure 4-7.

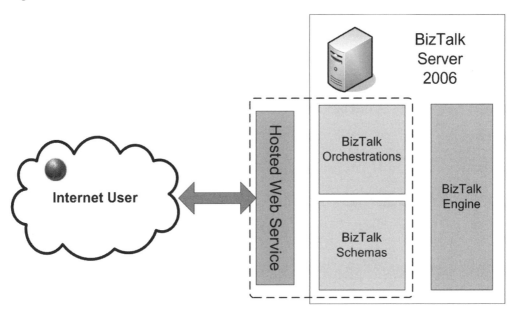

Figure 4-7. *Hosting orchestrations and schemas as web services*

You create your web services through the BizTalk Web Services Publishing Wizard, as shown in Figure 4-8.

Business Rule Composer

During the course of creating in-depth business integration services, you undoubtedly will build functionality known as *business rules*. Think of the rules engine as a way of enforcing corporate logic against your incoming and outgoing data. Does your company require that all incoming data be processed against a set of standardized criteria (taxation, inventory control, and minimum and maximum orders, and so on)? The business rules engine will efficiently tie in that ability to your BizTalk processes.

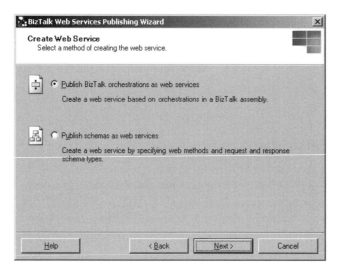

Figure 4-8. *Web Services Publishing Wizard*

The Microsoft Business Rule Composer provides an excellent interface for creating the necessary rules for your integration endeavors, as shown in Figure 4-9. You'll use the Rule Composer in Chapter 12.

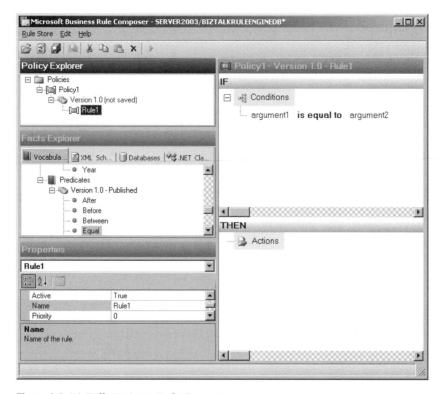

Figure 4-9. *BizTalk Business Rule Composer*

Rules Engine Deployment Wizard

As you create your unique business rules, the Rules Engine Deployment Wizard, shown in Figure 4-10, will help you push those rules out to the server, making them available for processing. We'll cover the business rules engine deployment process in Chapter 12.

Figure 4-10. *Rules Engine Deployment Wizard*

Health and Activity Tracking

Commonly referred to as HAT, the Health and Activity Tracking application allows you to analyze and debug messages that have made it into the tracking database. You'll use this application quite a bit when you're trying to trace the path that a particular message has taken or if you're attempting to troubleshoot a faulty orchestration. Out of the box, HAT has a few queries that you can use to find existing messages in the system, as shown in Figure 4-11.

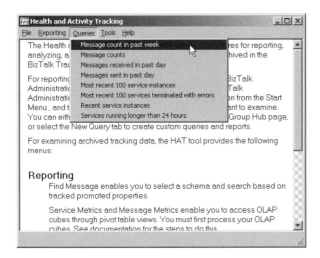

Figure 4-11. *Predefined tracking queries in HAT*

One of the handiest features of HAT is the ability to "step through" orchestrations, as shown in Figure 4-12.

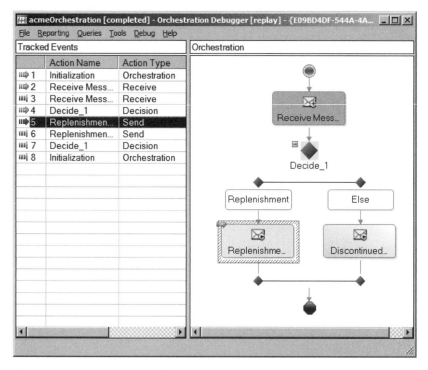

Figure 4-12. *Debugging an orchestration with HAT*

Tracking Profile Editor

The Tracking Profile Editor, shown in Figure 4-13, allows you tie BizTalk BAM activities to their server component counterparts (orchestrations, ports, and so on). We won't be using this particular application in this book. However, I encourage you to visit the BizTalk site (http://www.microsoft.com/biztalk) for more information after you have a good grasp on BAM activity creation and monitoring.

Visual Studio 2005 Tools

When you installed BizTalk Server 2006 in Chapter 3, you also installed the BizTalk project template. This is where you'll be constructing the multitude of BizTalk entities. You'll be making heavy use of the template throughout the book. If you start Visual Studio 2005, you'll find the application templates waiting for you, as shown in Figure 4-14.

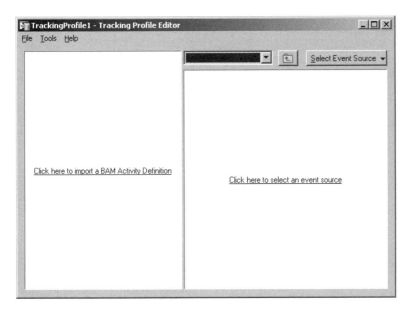

Figure 4-13. *Tracking Profile Editor*

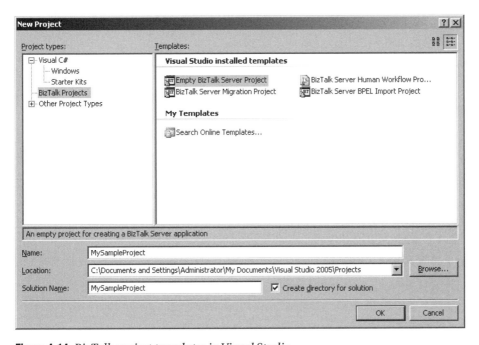

Figure 4-14. *BizTalk project templates in Visual Studio*

Once inside Visual Studio, right-clicking the project name and selecting Add New Item will lead you to yet another BizTalk template dialog box, as shown in Figure 4-15. It is here that you'll add the necessary integration tools to your project. We will cover a majority of those you see in Figure 4-15 as we progress through the book.

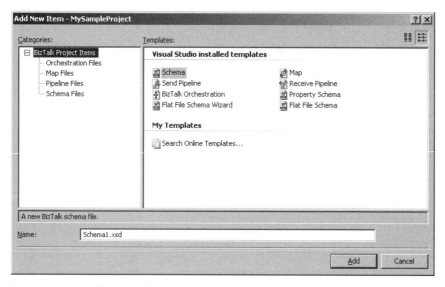

Figure 4-15. *BizTalk available artifacts in Visual Studio*

If you look on the View menu within Visual Studio 2005, you'll notice that you have an option for the BizTalk Explorer. As shown in Figure 4-16, this is an easy-access snap-in for Visual Studio, and you may find it handy for quick lookups. However, for most work, you'll probably want to leave the BizTalk Server Administration Console open and work from there. Still, it is nice to have the BizTalk Explorer within Visual Studio 2005 (despite the absence of the application view).

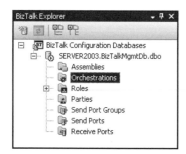

Figure 4-16. *BizTalk Explorer in Visual Studio*

SQL Server Database Changes

You'll notice right away that a few databases were added to your SQL Server box, as a result of your BizTalk installation. I'm bringing them to your attention so that you'll know what they represent and you'll be less inclined to delete them. For the record, you should steer clear (*really, really clear*) of manipulating the hard data within these databases. Because BizTalk lives and breathes from these particular storage entities, they become an essential part of the infrastructure. Bad things can happen when the BizTalk infrastructure is harmed. You could destroy BizTalk application functionality or, worse yet, lose important messages stored within the database.

You should find the databases listed in Table 4-1 (based on the BizTalk options installed) on your SQL Server.

Table 4-1. *SQL Server Databasess Added by BizTalk*

Database	Purpose
SSODB	Enterprise Single Sign-On database
BizTalkRuleEngineDB	Repository for your business rules
BizTalkMsgBoxDb	Storage for a multitude of BizTalk activities, notably messages
BizTalkMgmtDb	Database for server meta data
BizTalkHwsDb	Human Workflow Services storage database
BizTalkEdiDb	State data for the EDI adapter
BizTalkDTADb	BizTalk tracking engine storage
BizTalkStarSchema	Staging, dimension, and measure tables
BAMPrimaryImport	Raw tracking data for BAM
BAMArchive	Archive for older business activity
BAMAlertsNSMain	Notification services for BAM monitoring
BAMAlertsApplication	Alert information for BAM notifications

Summary

As you can see, BizTalk Server 2006 encompasses quite a few applications. Some you'll use quite a bit; a few you may never use. During the course of this book, you will become familiar with the core applications that you will use on a day-to-day basis when building your own custom integration systems. All of the products are worthy of follow-up when you've completed the book, and I encourage you to continue your education.

In the next chapter, we'll take a look at the next essential technology to the BizTalk world: the message.

CHAPTER 5

■ ■ ■

Message and Delivery

One of the terms that you've seen quite a bit of so far in this book is *message*. I'm sure that you've come to surmise that it is indeed integral to the world of BizTalk (especially since I emphasized that point in Chapter 1). And if you're like most people, you've also come to assume that it is strictly an XML file that you feed to your BizTalk Server system and let the Microsoft product work its magic. But there is so much more to BizTalk messaging and what constitutes a legitimate working integration message. In this chapter, we'll not only discuss what a message is, but how you get these items that are so necessary to your enterprise application.

What Is a Message?

Recently, I had to teach a lunch-and-learn session on BizTalk Server 2006, and one of the questions that came up was "What is a BizTalk message?" And I replied, "Anything." Of course, I was met with confused looks, and quickly qualified my response.

A BizTalk message is anything that you need it to be. If you can save it, send it, or serialize it, then it can be a message that is usable to the BizTalk system. If you wanted to send pictures to the BizTalk messaging system, you could do that. BizTalk will accept a lot of material. Is it practical and efficient to accept everything into the server? Of course not.

Most of you are well aware of traffic and storage concerns surrounding server usage. The debate of whether to store images in SQL Server database tables still rages on. So in all honesty, yes BizTalk can accept just about anything. But in the context of this book, what is practical and typical for the product? Let's first look at a fairly standard use-case scenario.

Messaging Scenario

For the sake of demonstration, let's say that you work for Acme Inc., which deals in auto parts. You have a back-end database where you store your parts inventory and a website that delivers the retail portion of your business to the world.

Recently, you've learned that one of your primary vendors, JoeBobs Mufflers, will be offering a daily update of the company's current deliverable stock with updated pricing. Your IT director has tasked you with integrating the vendor's delta update into your pricing model so that you're offering your customers the best deal on mufflers.

So you contact the IT department at JoeBobs, and you're told that they push a comma-separated-values (CSV) text file out to their FTP server every night. They'll create an account for you to log in and give you the appropriate rights to the file. But then the question hits you:

What do you do with that file? How will you retrieve it? How will you process the file and update the pricing model to reflect the changes? Figure 5-1 demonstrates the dilemma that you face when doing business with JoeBobs Mufflers.

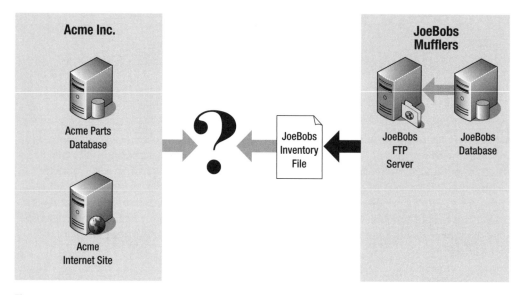

Figure 5-1. *Interaction problem with parts vendor*

I'm sure that you can already tell that, based on this scenario (and the fact that this is a BizTalk Server book), you'll be implementing the BizTalk Server product as a means of integrating with JoeBobs Mufflers, as shown in Figure 5-2. More to the point, the .csv file that JoeBob's IT department will distribute daily is your incoming message. Finally, an actual message to work with!

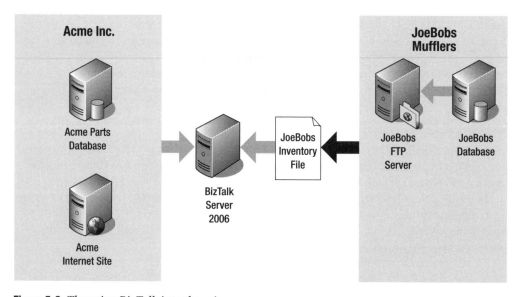

Figure 5-2. *Throwing BizTalk into the mix*

So in the current scenario, this CSV file is your message:

```
0112992,Big Honking Muffler,5,39.99
0112994,Loud Ignorant Muffler,7,29.99
0112996,Monster Truck Muffler,9,129.99
0122394,Motorcycle Muffler,3,29.99
```

Within BizTalk, you'll parse this file, convert it to XML (more on this in Chapter 7), and then process the contents based on your business needs.

Later, your favorite IT director asks, "Wouldn't it be neat if we could open up some of our business processes so that our vendors could notify us of a shipment, via the Internet?" Which is a fancy way of saying, "I'm telling you to make this happen. Have a nice day."

So the logical choice that you make is to create a web page for your vendors on a secured site that would allow them to post a message with an invoice number and ship date.

The basic concept is that you'll call a web service from your page that will forward a message to BizTalk via the web server, as illustrated in Figure 5-3.

JoeBob
Employee

Acme
Web
Application

Internet

Acme
Web
Service

Incoming
SOAP
Message

BizTalk
Server
2006

Figure 5-3. *Acme web interface flow*

In your new Internet-enabled project, the SOAP envelope (and contents) from the web service will now serve as your BizTalk message. You'll consume that SOAP package, process it, and update your database tables as needed.

The premise of both scenarios is to demonstrate that you can define a BizTalk message in a number of ways. It may be a SOAP package, a file sitting on an FTP server, an HTTP post, and many other things.

Common Types of Messages

Because of the diversity of BizTalk, I can't say that one message type or format is preferred by many over others. However, I can say that in my experience and conversations with others, I have found that a couple of formats, or message types, seem to pop up often:

XML files: As XML has become a strong player in the world of business integration, you would be hard-pressed to find a BizTalk developer who hasn't had to deal with the XML format. As I mentioned in Chapter 2, XML is a backbone of the BizTalk messaging system. Often, vendors or trading partners are willing to supply their content in a valid and verifiable XML format. This can make it substantially easier on you, especially if they supply the appropriate schema files as well. You'll work with XML quite a bit in the sample applications, in upcoming chapters.

Flat files: Whether the files are CSV, tab-delimited, or in a proprietary format, BizTalk is capable of processing them all. I've had the "pleasure" of working with some pretty strenuous flat-file formats (HL7 and EDI), and I've come to love the built-in tools that BizTalk provides for parsing these files.

In my humble opinion, these message formats seem to be the most popular in the integration world. But how do you get these messages into the system?

Message Delivery

I only want to scratch the surface of message delivery here, because later we'll be investigating BizTalk ports (Chapter 8), and I want to save some of the good stuff for that discussion. You should, however, understand that BizTalk is quite capable of assuming the leading role for a multitude of message-delivery systems.

In the two scenarios outlined earlier in the chapter, you were tasked to interact with your vendor via FTP and a web service. Those are just two of the many possibilities that you have with BizTalk, out of the box. By that, I mean that BizTalk supplies what are known as *adapters*, which are preconfigured to interface with a variety of platforms, right from the start, as shown in Figure 5-4.

As you can see, there are quite a few methods by which you can get your message into the system. What is really cool is that you're not limited to these methods. Microsoft and a few third-party entities are constantly releasing adapters that integrate with specialized systems (Siebel, SAP, EDI, and so on). And to top it all off, for those situations where it doesn't seem that any of the existing adapters do the trick, you can always create your own custom adapter.

Ultimately, you have an unlimited ability to get your messages in, process them, and send them on their way. How you integrate that ability into your business system becomes a key component in your overall architecture. Which brings me to the next topic in our brief discussion of messages and delivery: messaging patterns.

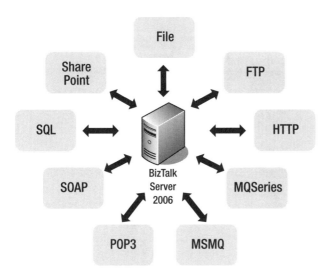

Figure 5-4. *Stock BizTalk adapters*

Message-Delivery Patterns

As you poke around the Internet, looking for help on BizTalk architecture, you will certainly come across a few common pattern phrases:

- Scatter-gather

- Request-reply

- Publish-subscribe

BizTalk developers, when discussing their particular messaging options, will often throw these terms around in conversation. Simply put, they describe the particular way in which their enterprise (or just BizTalk) consumes and produces their messages. The best way to understand these patterns is to think in terms of real-world examples, so let's do that.

Scatter-Gather

Suppose that your company, Acme Inc., is interested in the lowest prices offered for its muffler retail section. Your business users send a bid request to BizTalk, which in turn "scatters" the request to all of your vendors. Some may respond, and some may choose to pass on the request, as shown in Figure 5-5. BizTalk will then wait and "gather" those messages from the vendors that respond, process them, and pass them back to the business user. This is what the scatter-gather pattern will do for you. You'll use an aggregator pattern on the return trip to process the messages that come back, as described in the upcoming section on message-processing patterns.

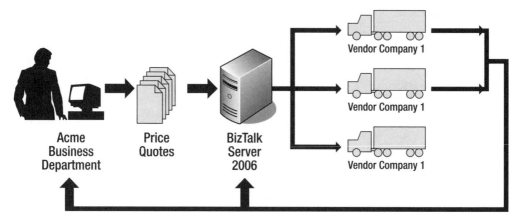

Figure 5-5. *Scatter-gather messaging pattern*

Request-Reply

To explain the request-reply pattern, we'll leave our friends and coworkers at Acme for a bit. With healthcare messaging, you are often constrained to a strict regimen of rules and guidelines for your message delivery and processing. One particular set of restrictions is the HL7 standard by which messages are composed, delivered, and consumed. Of interest here is the fact that when a healthcare organization submits a message to your BizTalk system, more often than not, it will want a reply indicating that you have received it (an ACK for successful acknowledgment, or NACK for the opposite). So BizTalk will receive an HL7 message as part of the request portion and will promptly notify the sender of receipt, as shown in Figure 5-6.

■**Note** HL7 (Health Level 7) is a nonprofit group whose goal is to standardize the way that healthcare organizations interface and trade information. The HL7 standard is the framework by which the various rules and guidelines are enforced.

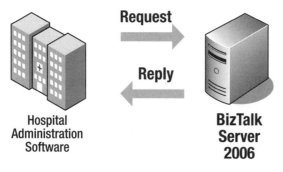

Figure 5-6. *Request-reply pattern*

Publish-Subscribe

One of the more prevalent patterns out on the Web is the publish-subscribe pattern (also known as pub/sub). In this chapter's scenarios, Acme has asked you to deliver the pub/sub pattern. After hours of research, you come to the realization that you're simply going to push (publish) your generated file (message) out to a flat file location that JoeBobs application server has rights to access. JoeBobs server has a process running that monitors (subscribes to) the file folder, as shown in Figure 5-7. When a message appears, they'll pick it up and run with it. We'll use this particular pattern in a few examples throughout the course of the book, as it is the easiest and fastest to implement.

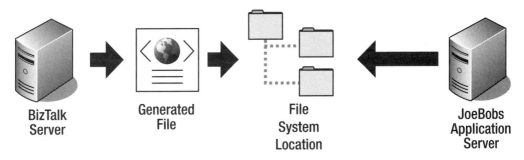

Figure 5-7. *Publish-subscribe pattern*

Message-Processing Patterns

I've split the following patterns out, away from delivery patterns, because they are geared towards what BizTalk does with the messages received, rather than the method by which they arrived. Here again, these are just ambiguous concepts, and I'm sure that if you searched long enough, you would find at least three differing meanings for each. But I'm going to settle on generalized descriptions so that you at least understand the basic premise. And I'm also going to concern this section with what I feel to be the three most popular message-processing patterns:

- Aggregator
- First in/first out
- Splitter

Aggregator

The aggregator pattern does exactly what its name implies: It aggregates any given number of messages into one primary message for processing within BizTalk. As shown in the scatter-gather illustration (Figure 5-5), the business department will be waiting for a multitude of messages from the product vendors. As they generate bids and submit them to your system, BizTalk will collect them (aggregate) and compile the information to a single vendor bid message that your business processes can then use to make important financial decisions. Figure 5-8 shows the generalized pattern by which the vendor messages are routed into the BizTalk system.

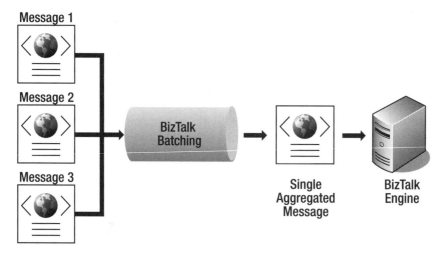

Figure 5-8. *Aggregation pattern*

First In/First Out

Think of the first in/first out pattern as the BizTalk car wash. When you take your ride down to the local automated wash-and-dry, the cars are washed in the order in which they roll into the machine. Provided a catastrophic failure of equipment does not occur, if you're the first guy in, you'll be the first guy out. You could certainly throw the car in reverse and delay the process, but if there is someone in line behind you, I can almost guarantee that you'll still be the first guy out, most likely by force. The same applies to BizTalk first in/first out messaging (also known as FIFO). Messages are dealt with as they arrived and delivered in the appropriate order, as shown in Figure 5-9. This is *not* a default pattern with BizTalk. To get this kind of functionality, you need to configure for it.

Figure 5-9. *First in/first out pattern*

Splitter

One of the more useful features that we have available is the ability to take a single file with multiple line items and separate it into individual, processable, messages. For instance, say that at Acme, you receive an order for products via a single XML file that has been posted on your system. Within that single file, you have this:

```
Customer Name
Billing Info
Ordered Item 1
Ordered Item 2
Ordered Item 3
```

You would like to split each ordered item out into its own individual file so that you can bounce it around the various departments for inventory check, shipping calculation, and procurement. In this situation, you'll split the incoming message, as shown in Figure 5-10, and it will work as expected.

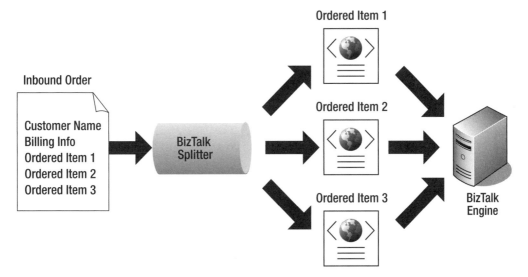

Figure 5-10. *Splitter pattern*

Summary

We've established that a message is really anything that you want it to be, within reason, of course. You still need to adhere to general best practices when it comes to server traffic and storage, but you understand that BizTalk is rather generous in what it will allow you to process. As you'll see in the various applications that you'll build in the chapters to come, your primary messages will be XML and flat-file based text files that you'll parse, validate, and process. In the next chapter, you'll begin that process by understanding how you define those messages that you'll use. By defining them, you'll be able to ensure that you're getting the right data in the right format. You'll also get a chance to, finally(!), fire up Visual Studio 2005 and work with this crazy BizTalk thing.

CHAPTER 6

■■■

Schemas

In Chapter 2, we took a look at the structure of schemas and how they relate to an XML file. Schemas not only describe the structure of an XML file, but they also can place constraints on the data that is contained within the file. Why is this important? Well, imagine that you've recently bought a model rocket kit online. Your kit shows up, and you eagerly begin construction of the space-bound ship. However, you get to the last step and realize that the manufacturer has neglected to supply the nose cone. So you're left with a rocket-propelled toilet paper tube and *not* your intergalactic starship. The product is useless for the task for which you purchased it. The same can be said about file schemas. They are the parts list for the files with which they are associated. If the right parts or data are not included with the targeted file, then the file is useless for the task in which it is being consumed. In BizTalk terms, we call this a failed validation of the file.

In this chapter, you will use Visual Studio and the BizTalk Schema Editor to create a few schemas that describe two different file formats: an XML file and a CSV flat file. You'll want to have a firm grasp on schema creation before moving on to the next chapter, as the schema-generation process is essential to success when dealing with BizTalk.

An XML Schema

In this first example, you'll build the schema file within Visual Studio 2005 for an XML file that does not exist yet. You'll build the blueprint for the file, and then create a sample file, generated by the BizTalk Schema Editor. But first, let's discuss what kind of data you want to transfer and/or validate.

Back at Acme Inc., you've been asked to develop some messaging standards for your ordering process. Having read the first five chapters of this book, you now understand that before you begin that process, you need to establish the structure of your data. Your XML file schemas will be the foundation of the BizTalk messaging process, and fortunately, given the ease of editing, you can revisit them later (as needed) to mold and shape them into a production-worthy product.

So you hack out a few requirements and find that your first component, the `itemOrder.xml` file, is pretty lightweight. You're interested in only particular fields when you submit the file for replenishment:

```
CustomerName
CustomerAddress1
CustomerAddress2
CustomerCity
```

```
CustomerState
CustomerZip
CustomerContactName
CustomerContactPhone
OrderedItemProductNumber
OrderedItemProductQuantity
OrderedItemProductPrice
```

So you'll need to build this structure into your XML schema.

Creating the XML Schema File

The first task is to create the schema file. We'll use Visual Studio 2005 as our tool of choice.

1. Start Visual Studio 2005.

2. Create a new project by clicking File ➤ New ➤ Project.

3. Choose to create an Empty BizTalk Server Project, enter Chapter6 as a project name, and set the location as C:\acme\chapter 6, as shown in Figure 6-1. Then click OK.

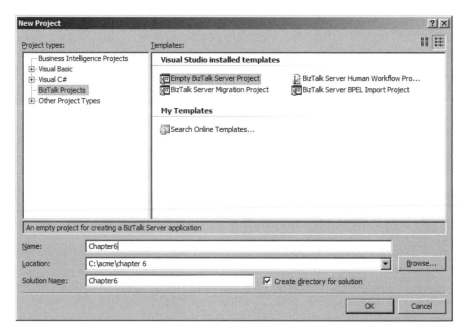

Figure 6-1. *Creating the Chapter6 project*

4. In the Solution Explorer, right-click the project name and select Add ➤ New Item, as shown in Figure 6-2.

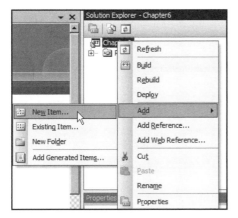

Figure 6-2. *Adding a new item to your solution*

5. Select the Schema Files node in the left panel, and then select Schema in the right panel. Save the file as Order.xsd, as shown in Figure 6-3. Click Add to close the dialog box.

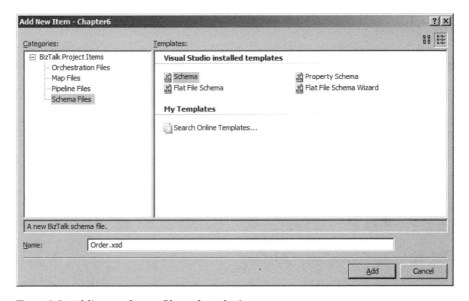

Figure 6-3. *Adding a schema file to the solution*

Now that you have added the schema file to the solution, Visual Studio will open the file in the Schema Editor. As you can see, you have the XML nodes to the left and the actual XML text to the right, as shown in Figure 6-4.

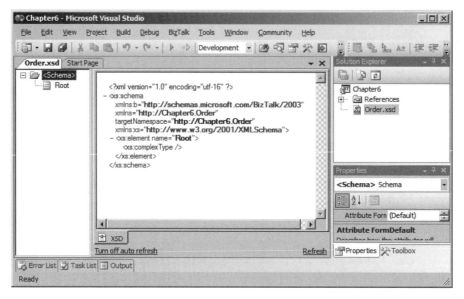

Figure 6-4. *The XML schema file in the Schema Editor*

Creating the XML Schema

By default, Visual Studio has added an initial Root node for you. However, that does not really match your data goal, so you'll need to rename that before you begin adding anything else below it. This schema file will be responsible for validating (or describing) only a single order at a time, so you'll name the root node Order.

1. Right-click the Root node and select Rename, as shown in Figure 6-5.

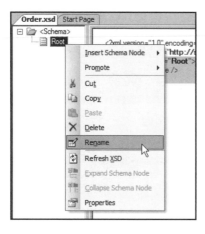

Figure 6-5. *Renaming the root node*

2. Modify the name so that it reads Order.

Adding Nodes

As you would expect, you need to add the rest of your nodes, to match your expected structure.

1. Right-click the Order node and select Insert Schema Node, as shown in Figure 6-6. You can see that you have a multitude of options available on this context menu. In this example, you're only interested in Child Field Element, so select that as the node to insert.

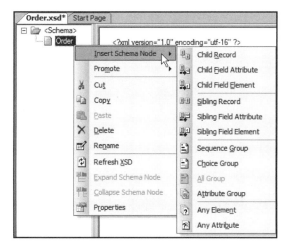

Figure 6-6. *Options for inserting schema nodes*

■**Note** Remember the basic difference between a record and a field? A *record* can have other nested elements below it. The Order node is a record node. A *field* cannot have nested elements. Typically, you'll use this for your data fields.

---

2. Within the highlighted text, type CustomerName, and then click off the node to save your edit. You should now have a new child element and the appropriate XML schema text, as shown in Figure 6-7.

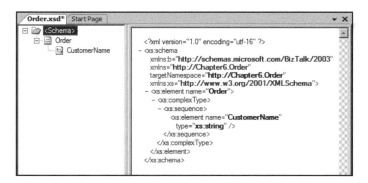

Figure 6-7. *The new child element*

3. Repeat steps 1 and 2 to add the following child fields to the schema:

- CustomerAddress1

- CustomerAddress2

- CustomerCity

- CustomerState

- CustomerZip

- CustomerContactName

- CustomerContactPhone

- OrderedItemProductNumber

After you've added the listed fields, your schema should look like Figure 6-8. Notice that you did not add the Quantity and Price fields yet. We need to discuss a thing or two before you add those into the mix.

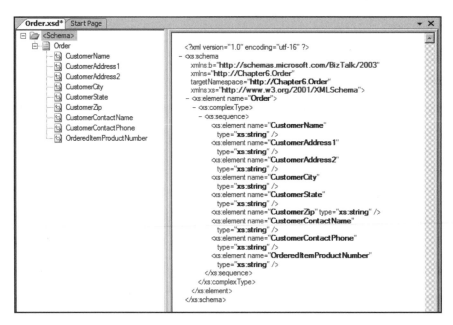

Figure 6-8. *Your current schema file*

Setting the Data Type

Now that you've added all of those fields, did you notice that they have something in common? They're all string types, which is okay for the particular fields that they represent. However, you still need to add the Price and Quantity fields into the schema, and it would make sense to have those fields in the particular type that would facilitate any number of math functions against them. So you'll need to add the last two remaining elements and change their data types.

1. Insert another Child Field Element and name it `OrderItemProductQuantity`. Click off the node to save the edit.

2. Highlight the new node, right-click and select Properties to bring up the Properties window.

3. Scroll down (if needed) until you find the Data Type property. Change the type to `xs:int`, as shown in Figure 6-9.

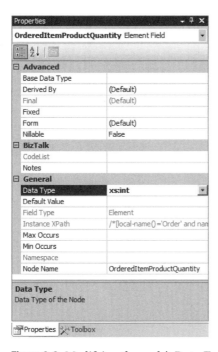

Figure 6-9. *Modifying the node's Data Type property*

4. Right-click the root node and insert another Child Field Element.

5. Change the name of the element to `OrderedItemProductPrice`.

6. In the Properties window, change the Data Type to `xs:decimal`.

Your completed schema should be as shown in Figure 6-10.

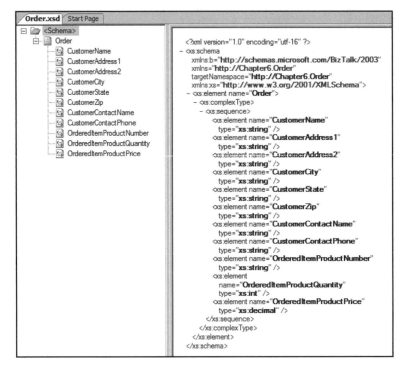

Figure 6-10. *The completed Order schema*

Creating a Sample XML File

One of the benefits of creating a schema with Visual Studio and the BizTalk Schema Editor is that you can use that schema file to create a sample XML file. This can be incredibly useful for testing other BizTalk functionality when you don't have a vendor-supplied sample data file.

1. Right-click Order.xsd in the Solution Explorer and select Properties.

2. Set the Output Instance Filename to C:\acme\chapter6\sampleOrder.xml, as shown in Figure 6-11. This tells BizTalk where to store the file it will generate. You could, of course, choose another location—just remember where the file resides. Click OK to close the dialog box.

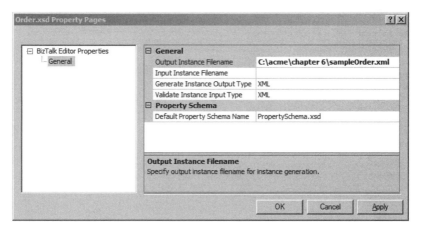

Figure 6-11. *Schema Property Pages dialog box*

3. Right-click Order.xsd in the Solution Explorer again and, this time, select Generate Instance, as shown in Figure 6-12.

Figure 6-12. *Generating the XML file*

After a second or two, your file will be generated and dropped into its designated folder. If you switch over to the Output window, you'll see a link that you can click, as shown in Figure 6-13. Clicking it opens the fresh and exciting XML file within Visual Studio, as shown in Figure 6-14.

Figure 6-13. *Generation output message*

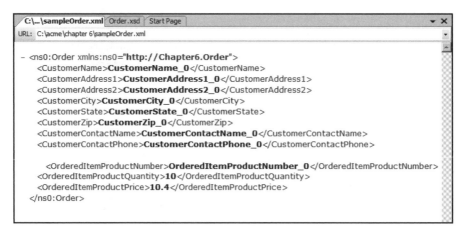

Figure 6-14. *The sample XML file*

You'll notice that Visual Studio has been kind enough to supply you with the appropriate data for the data types that you specified: Your string fields have character data, and your numeric fields contain numbers.

So you've created an XML file from scratch. And that has some practicality to it. But I'm quite sure that in your BizTalk work, you'll find that you have the XML data file, but not the schema. Fear not, for help is on the way!

Generating an XML Schema

Before you generate the requisite schema, you first need to have the XML file on which you will base your schema. Then you can have the Schema Editor create the schema for you.

1. Create the following file and save it in the chapter 6 folder that you created earlier.

```
<InventoryItem>
<ItemName>Brake Pads</ItemName>
<ItemPartNumber>01003204</ItemPartNumber>
<QuantityOnHand>23</QuantityOnHand>
<ReOrderQuantity>10</ReOrderQuantity>
</InventoryItem>
```

2. Right-click the project and select Add ➤ Add Generated Items, as shown in Figure 6-15.

Figure 6-15. *Adding a generated schema file*

3. Select Generate Schemas in both the left and right panels, as shown in Figure 6-16, and then click Add to continue.

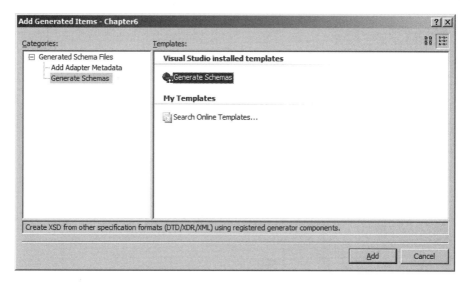

Figure 6-16. *Selecting the Generate Schemas option*

4. If Well-Formed XML is not selected as the Document Type, select it in the drop-down list. Click the browse button and find the XML file that you created and saved earlier, as shown in Figure 6-17. Click OK to continue.

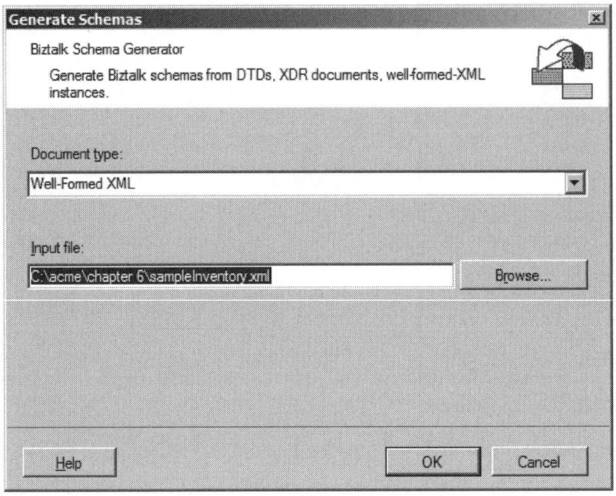

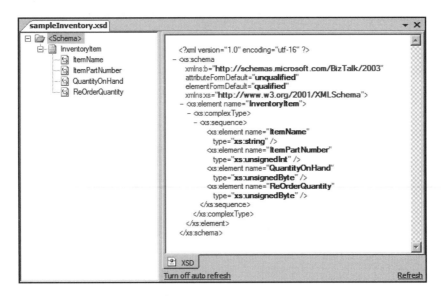

Figure 6-17. *Finding and adding the XML file*

After a moment or two, you'll have a brand-new schema in the Schema Editor, as shown in Figure 6-18, just waiting to be put to good use.

Figure 6-18. *Your generated schema*

As you poke around with the new schema file, you'll notice that the interpreter almost got the data types correct. Nice try, but you'll have to do some tweaking to get the types you need. The Add Generated Items feature is powerful, but it may not eliminate all of the work that you need to perform to have a fully functional and meaningful schema for your BizTalk project. Fortunately, with the Schema Editor, it's a snap to change the data types on the fly.

A Flat File Schema

As many of you already know, it is quite possible that you will be integrating data from a variety of sources, and some of those sources may not have adopted XML as their data structure. Perhaps their system was designed and implemented prior to the XML revolution. Regardless of the reason, it may fall to you to import their data on their terms and structure. One common format that we all find ourselves dealing with is the flat file.

Flat files come in all shapes and flavors: comma-separated, tab-delimited, pipe-separated, or just plain-old text in a single string. The list of available file construction methods can go on for quite some time. Fortunately with BizTalk, we have the tools to fight the madness. The Flat File Schema Wizard allows you to virtually "dissect" the incoming file and end with a manageable schema that is quick and easy to validate.

Creating the Flat File

Let's first create a sample flat file that is comma-separated. You'll use the previous item order structure, but adhere to the CSV format. You'll also be adding more than one line item to the file.

Here is the structure revisited:

```
CustomerName
CustomerAddress1
CustomerAddress2
CustomerCity
CustomerState
CustomerZip
CustomerContactName
CustomerContactPhone
OrderedItemProductNumber
OrderedItemProductQuantity
OrderedItemProductPrice
```

1. Create a new text file named `orderFlatFile.txt`.

2. Enter the following text data in it, pressing Enter at the end of the Price field, so you have *two* lines (even though they're shown as four lines here, to fit on the page):

   ```
   Joe Smith,101 Nowhere Lane,Apt 123,Grand Rapids,Michigan,49503,
   Joe Smith,616-555-1212,29993933,1,39.99
   Bob Jones,3131 Crazy Road,,Flint,Michigan,49506,
   Martha Jones,810-555-2121,399959599,2,19.99
   ```

3. Save your file in the `chapter 6` folder.

Creating the Flat File Schema

Now that you have a flat file, you're ready to try out the Flat File Schema Wizard.

1. Start Visual Studio 2005.

2. Right-click the project name in the Solution Explorer and select Add ➤ Add New Item.

3. Select Schema Files in the left panel and Flat File Schema Wizard in the right panel. Name the file `orderFlatFile.xsd`, as shown in Figure 6-19. Click Add to continue.

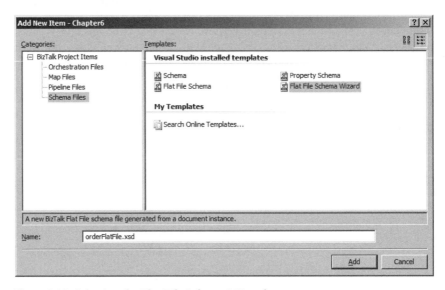

Figure 6-19. *Selecting the Flat File Schema Wizard*

4. The Welcome dialog box appears. Click Next to continue.

5. The Flat File Schema Information dialog box appears. Use the Browse button to locate your file. Set the Record Name to `Orders`, as shown in Figure 6-20. Accept the default settings for the Target Namespace and Code Page options. Click Next to continue.

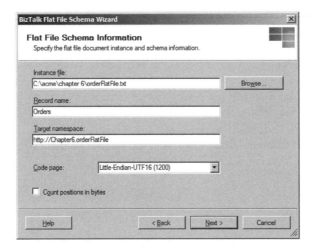

Figure 6-20. *Supplying the flat file schema information*

6. Your next task is to select the actual text for which you would like to create a schema. In the current scenario, that would be all of it. Use your mouse to drag over all of the text to select it, as shown in Figure 6-21. Then click Next to continue.

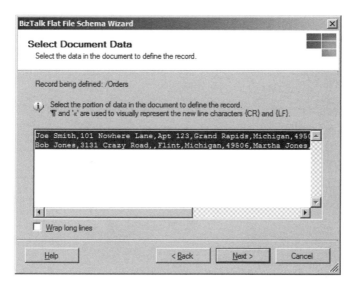

Figure 6-21. *Selecting the appropriate text*

7. The wizard asks how you would like to portion out your flat file. You have the option of using delimiters or relative positions as the segment separators. Select the delimiter option, as shown in Figure 6-22, and then click Next to continue.

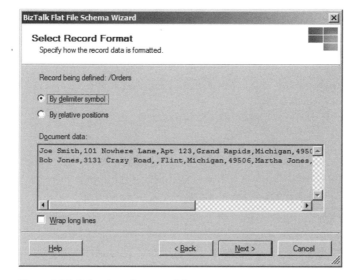

Figure 6-22. *Selecting the record format*

8. You now need to specify the delimiter used in your text file. This step deals with how you differentiate between each data row. You used a carriage return/line feed (CR/LF) at the end of each line to terminate the row. So, in the Child Delimiter drop-down list, select {CR}{LF}, as shown in Figure 6-23. Then click Next.

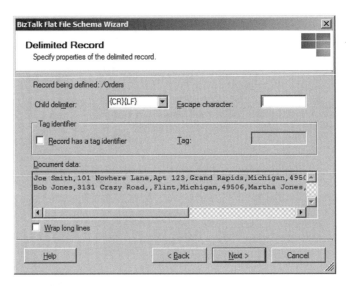

Figure 6-23. *Specifying the delimiter symbol*

▪**Note** I know that some of you noticed the Tag Identifier section of the Delimited Record dialog box and are anxiously awaiting some explanation. Suppose that you have a flat file that prefixes each row as shown in the following two code lines (they're spread across four lines here, to fit on the page, but we're talking about a pair of lines in a text editor):

```
_OrdJoe Smith,101 Nowhere Lane,Apt 123,Grand Rapids,Michigan,49503,
Joe Smith,616-555-1212,29993933,1,39.99
_OrdBob Jones,3131 Crazy Road,,Flint,Michigan,49506,
Martha Jones,810-555-2121,399959599,2,19.99
```

As you can see, there is an _Ord set of characters at the beginning of each row. With your tag identifier, you can let the wizard know right up front that you're interested in separating that particular information, rather than having it be included with the first segment (which, in this case, is the Name field).

---

9. You now need to tell the wizard which rows are repeating, as shown in Figure 6-24. Change the Element Name on the first row to something meaningful, like OrderDetail. Set the Element Type on the first row to Repeating Record.

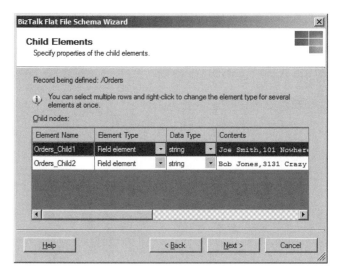

Figure 6-24. *Specifying the row information*

10. Because the other line item(s) are simply repeating the same format as the first, you need to set the Element Type to Ignore, as shown in Figure 6-25, so that BizTalk will simply skip that data when generating the schema. Remember that you're specifying the schema layout, and not dictating which data gets accepted or rejected. This process has nothing to do with the data as content, but rather the structure of the document as a whole. Click Next to continue.

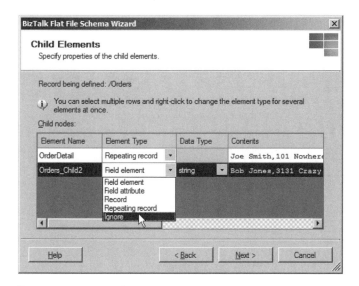

Figure 6-25. *Setting the repeating rows to Ignore*

11. BizTalk now recognizes that you have a record that is in need of further configuration, as shown in Figure 6-26. This will give you an opportunity to describe to the wizard how you would like to have each line item parsed. Highlight OrderDetail (if it is not already highlighted) and click Next to continue.

Figure 6-26. *Further configuration needed*

12. You're asked to specify the particular data again, as shown in Figure 6-27. Bear in mind that you're only interested in declaring schema information for a single line item, so select the first item (highlighted by default) and click Next to continue.

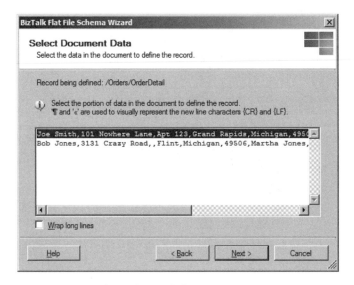

Figure 6-27. *Specifying the single line item*

13. Again, you'll be using a delimiter symbol for parsing (the comma), so accept the delimiter option, as shown in Figure 6-28, and click Next to continue.

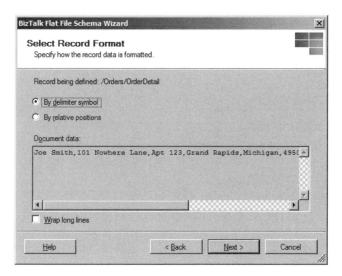

Figure 6-28. *Specifying the delimiter option*

14. In the Delimited Record dialog box, select the comma from the list of child delimiters, as shown in Figure 6-29. Click Next to continue.

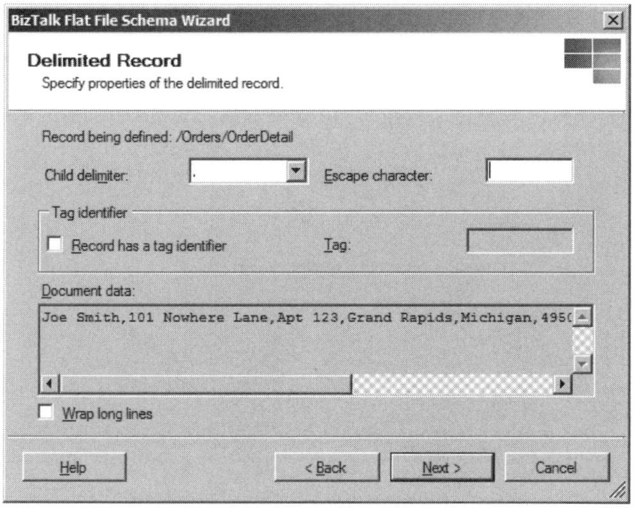

Figure 6-29. *Selecting the comma for a delimiter*

15. Finally, you get to declare the individual segments! The Child Elements dialog box, as shown (expanded) in Figure 6-30, allows you to declare the element name, element type, and data type for each segment. Because you're creating all field elements, modify only the element name and the data types, as follows:

- CustomerName: string

- CustomerAddress1: string

- CustomerAddress2: string

- CustomerCity: string

- CustomerState: string

- CustomerZip: string

- CustomerContactName: string

- CustomerContactPhone: string

- OrderedItemProductNumber: string

- OrderedItemProductQuantity: int

- OrderedItemProductPrice: decimal

▪**Caution** Don't forget to set the data types for the quantity and price elements. They might try to sneak through as strings, and that could create issues when you attempt to apply math functions against the data later.

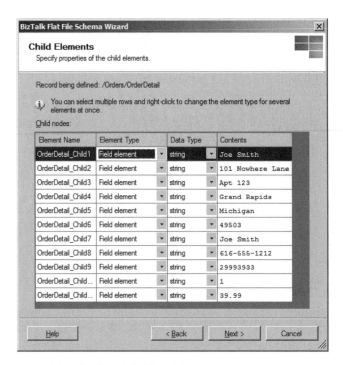

Figure 6-30. *The list of child elements*

16. Your child elements list should look like Figure 6-31. Click Next to continue.

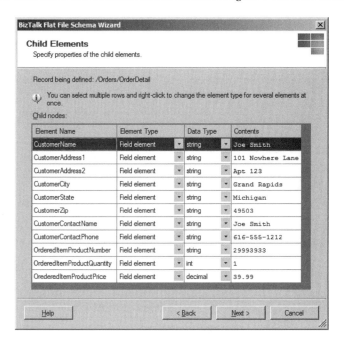

Figure 6-31. *Modified element names and types*

17. The wizard shows you that you have no further detail rows that are in need of modification. If you did, those rows would be shown in solid font, rather than grayed out, as they are in Figure 6-32. Click the Finish button.

Figure 6-32. *All of the schema elements are covered.*

You now have a working flat file schema for your orders file, complete with functionality for multiple line items, as needed.

As you scroll through the schema in the BizTalk Schema Editor, as shown in Figure 6-33, you'll be able to identify each of the fields and their corresponding data types. This schema is ready for action!

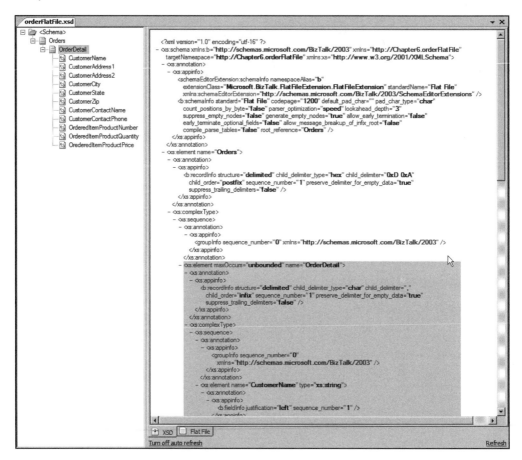

Figure 6-33. *The complete flat file schema*

Summary

In this chapter, we rapidly created two different types of schemas that can be used in a variety of application processes within BizTalk Server. XML and flat file schemas are quite prevalent in the world of integration transformations, and you'll use them often. Fortunately for the BizTalk community, the new Flat File Schema Wizard provides a quick and effortless method of building a schema capable of parsing a multitude of formats. I encourage you to try the wizard with different formats and structures to really get a feel for the tool as you move forward with your BizTalk studies.

In the next chapter, you'll have an opportunity to put these schemas to use with the BizTalk Mapper. You'll see how you can start the data transformation cycle by simply connecting elements.

CHAPTER 7

■■■

Mapping

The previous chapter discussed how cool schemas can be and how easy it is to mock one up in Visual Studio 2005. As you progress with your BizTalk training, you'll find that schemas become a necessary component for describing messages within the various integration processes. One of those processes that you'll find yourself doing quite a bit is mapping the fields of one schema to another distinct schema. In this chapter, we'll explore BizTalk mapping, both the concept and the tool, the BizTalk Mapper.

The BizTalk Mapping Concept

As you begin your production-level work, you'll often find that the messages coming into your messaging processes are not mapped appropriately for the business logic that you must apply to them. Similarly, you may have data leaving your enterprise that does not match the qualifications of a consuming trading partner. This is where BizTalk mapping steps in to save the day. You have the ability to add an all-important step to the message cycle by introducing *schema maps*.

Figure 7-1 illustrates a simple mapping pattern. If you build an XML schema (as discussed in Chapter 6) and develop the appropriate XML destination schema, you can map the results to the desired XML output.

Figure 7-1. *Simple mapping pattern*

As an example, suppose that you have an incoming XML file with some simple customer profile information: name, address, city, state, and ZIP code. As shown in Figure 7-2, based on the structure of the XML source document, you generate an XML schema file to represent the layout of the incoming data. The fields in the source XML schema are then mapped to the destination XML schema, and when the map is applied to the incoming data, the desired XML output is produced.

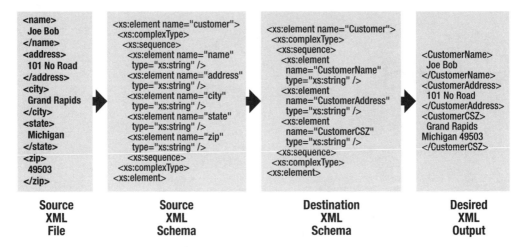

Figure 7-2. *Messaging pattern with source information*

Figure 7-3 shows the map file for this example in Visual Studio 2005. Now you'll learn how to work with the BizTalk Mapper to create schema maps.

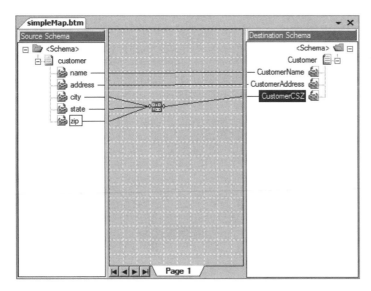

Figure 7-3. *A simple BizTalk schema map*

The BizTalk Mapper

The easiest way to understand BizTalk mapping is simply to fire up Visual Studio and get to building a schema map.

Creating the Source and Destination Schemas

To get started, you need to create a directory for this chapter and save an appropriate input XML file in that directory. Then you can generate your source and destination schemas. You're not going to do anything extravagant quite yet. You'll just move data from one field to another.

1. Create a directory for the project: `c:\acme\chapter 7`.

2. Create the following XML file in Notepad (or the XML editor of your choice):

```
<Customer>
<name>Joe Bob</name>
<address>101 No Road</address>
<city>Grand Rapids</city>
<state>Michigan</state>
<zip>49503</zip>
</Customer>
```

3. Save the XML file as `inputCustomer.xml` in your new `chapter 7` directory.

4. Start a new instance of Visual Studio 2005.

5. Create an empty BizTalk project and save it in the `chapter 7` folder.

6. Right-click the project name and select Add ➤ Add Generated Item.

7. Select Generate Schemas in both panes, and then click Add to continue.

8. You'll be asked to find and select the XML file that you created and saved earlier. Click the Browse button to locate your file, as shown in Figure 7-4, and then click OK. After a moment, you should have an `.xsd` file ready for action, as shown in Figure 7-5.

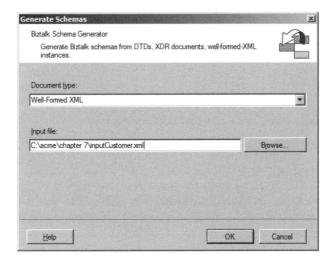

Figure 7-4. *Locating your XML file*

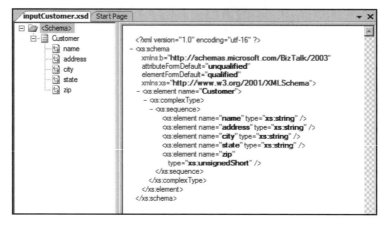

Figure 7-5. *The source schema file*

9. Right-click the project name and select Add ➤ New Item.

10. Select Schema Files in the left pane and Schema in the right pane. Name your file `destinationSchema.xsd`, and then click Add.

11. Change the root node of the schema file to `Contact` and add two child field elements: `Name` and `State`. Your new schema should look like Figure 7-6.

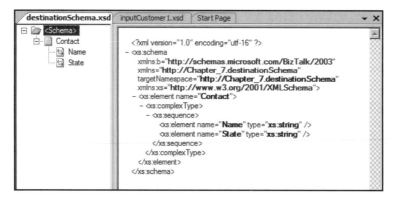

Figure 7-6. *Adding the appropriate elements to the destination schema*

Creating the Schema Map

Now it's time to create a real-life BizTalk schema map. In practice, you would typically create separate projects for schemas and for maps, but for this example, you're just going to throw your map into the same project as the schema files.

1. Right-click the project name and select Add ➤ New Item.

2. Select Map Files on the left, and then Map on the right.

3. Name the map `simpleMap.btm`.

After the map has been added to the project, you'll be presented with the Mapper, as shown in Figure 7-7.

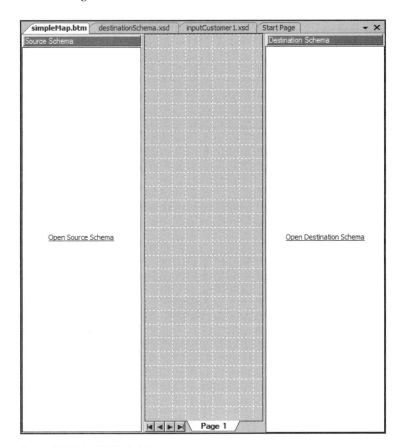

Figure 7-7. *The BizTalk Mapper*

Adding the Schemas

Within the IDE, you have three primary panels from which to work. The left and right sides, as you have already surmised, are for the appropriate schemas. The center panel is an area where you can manipulate how mappings are made by using BizTalk functoids (as explained later in this chapter).

Let's start by loading the source and destination schemas.

1. Click the Open Source Schema link in the left panel of the IDE, and expand the Schemas node until you can find and add the Chapter_7.inputCustomer schema, as shown in Figure 7-8.

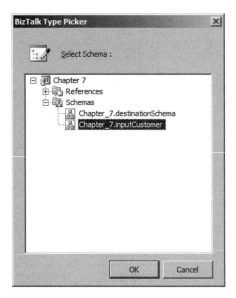

Figure 7-8. *Selecting the source schema*

2. After the schema has loaded, right-click the Schema header in the left panel and select Expand Tree Node. All of the nodes for the customer schema should now be visible.

3. Click the Open Destination Schema link in the right panel and add the Chapter_7.destinationSchema that you created earlier.

4. Right-click the Schema header in the right panel and select Expand Tree Node.

Associating Schema Elements

Mapping in the Visual Studio 2005 environment is quite easy. You simply highlight the node, and then drag it across the panels to the destination node, as shown in Figure 7-9.

Once you've connected the source node to the destination node, the association between the two elements has been established.

1. Connect the name node to the corresponding Name node in the destination schema.

2. Connect the state node to the corresponding State node in the destination schema. Your map should look like Figure 7-10.

Now that all of the fields are mapped, your next step is to test the map.

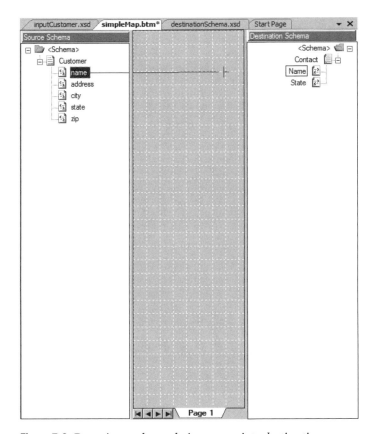

Figure 7-9. *Dragging nodes to their appropriate destination*

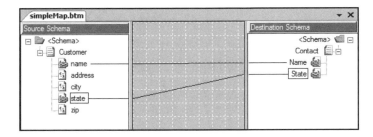

Figure 7-10. *Two fields mapped and ready*

Testing the Map

Before you can test your map, you need to associate an inbound XML file with the properties of the map.

1. Right-click the map name in the Solution Explorer and select Properties.

2. Find and associate your `inputCustomer.xml` file with the Input Instance Filename, as shown in Figure 7-11.

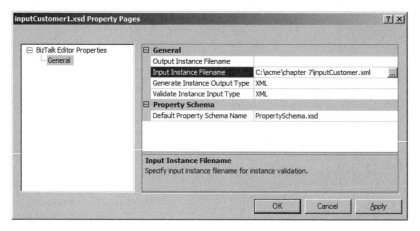

Figure 7-11. *Adding the input file name for testing*

3. Right-click the map name in the Solution Explorer and select Test Map, as shown in Figure 7-12.

Figure 7-12. *Testing the new map*

4. BizTalk will now use the inputCustomer.xml file as the sample data and "apply" it to the structure of the map. In a moment, the processing results will pop up, as shown in Figure 7-13. Ctrl-click the output file name (simpleMap_output.xml) to see the results, as shown in Figure 7-14.

The results are exactly as planned. You mapped the two fields, and two fields were delivered.

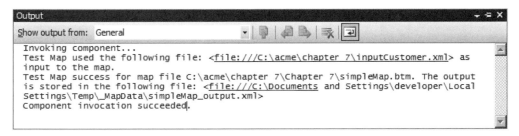

Figure 7-13. *Results listing*

Figure 7-14. *Viewing the successful test results*

Now as cool as that is, it's not really where the power of the BizTalk Mapper lies. One of the more powerful aspects of the tool is the usage of what Microsoft calls *functoids*—a goofy name, but a very strong set of tools.

BizTalk Functoids

With BizTalk Mapper functoids, you can perform a variety of simple or complex computational or manipulative tasks. You may have noticed as you were poking around with the Mapper that a toolbox was added as part of the project, as shown in Figure 7-15.

As you flip through each of the tree nodes, you'll notice that there are *a lot* of functoids. This is an amazing technology when you think about it. You can apply programming-like functions to your incoming data.

Here, you'll work through an example and try out a few functoids. I won't cover all of them, because that would take several chapters. You'll find that they're easy to use, and you'll want to experiment with them on your own. You can find the appropriate functoid implementation guidelines in the BizTalk Documentation (Start ➤ Programs ➤ Microsoft BizTalk Server 2006).

Figure 7-15. *The BizTalk Mapper Toolbox window*

Setting Up the Map

First, you need a map to manipulate. So, you need to start a new project, create an XML source file, and generate the source and destination schemas, as in the previous example.

1. Start a new instance of Visual Studio 2005.

2. Create a new Empty BizTalk Project and save it as Chapter7Advanced.

3. Create an XML file with the following content and save it as orderFile.xml:

```
<Order>
<CustomerFirstName>Joe </CustomerFirstName>
<CustomerLastName>Smith</CustomerLastName>
<OrderedItemQuantity>4</OrderedItemQuantity>
<OrderedItemPrice>12.99</OrderedItemPrice>
</Order>
```

4. Right-click the project name and select Add ➤ Add Generated Items.

5. Select Generate Schemas in both the left and right panes. Click Add to continue.

6. Find and add the orderFile.xml file when asked for the input file, as shown in Figure 7-16.

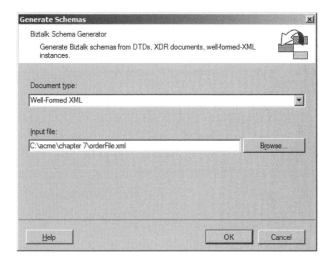

Figure 7-16. *Selecting your new orderFile.xml file*

7. After the schema has finished loading, modify the quantity Data Type property to xs:int. You want to keep it consistent with previous examples.

8. Right-click the project name and select Add ➤ New Item.

9. Select Schema Files on the left and Schema on the right. Save your file as orderDestination.xsd.

10. After the Schema Editor has loaded, rename the root node to InboundOrder.

11. Add two child field elements with the appropriate data types: CustomerName as xs:string, and OrderValue as xs:decimal. Your final schema should be as shown in Figure 7-17.

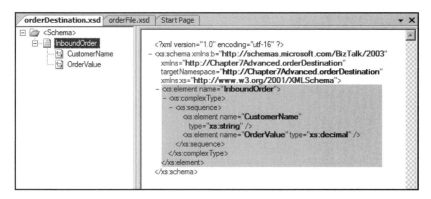

Figure 7-17. *The completed destination schema*

12. Right-click the project name and select Add ➤ New Item.

13. Select Map Files on the left and then Map on the right.

14. Save your map as `order.btm` and click OK to continue.

15. After the BizTalk Mapper has loaded, add the appropriate source and destination schema files, as you did in the previous example.

16. Expand both node trees, so that all nodes are now visible, as shown in Figure 7-18.

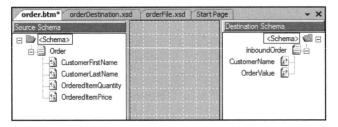

Figure 7-18. *The new map ready for manipulation*

Mapping with Functoids

To use a functoid, you drag it from the toolbox to the gridded area of the Mapper (the center pane). In this example, you're going to use functoids to accomplish two separate tasks. You'll first concatenate the customer's name so that it will read first name, space, last name. Then you'll multiply the quantity times the price to get the order value.

Using the String Concatenate Functoid

Let's get started with the String Concatenate functoid.

1. In the Mapper toolbox, click the String Functoids node and find the String Concatenate functoid, as shown in Figure 7-19.

Figure 7-19. *The String Concatenate functoid*

2. Click and drag the functoid out to the gridded center pane of the Mapper.

3. Click and drag CustomerFirstName in the source schema out to (and attaching to) the String Concatenate functoid in the center pane.

4. Click and drag CustomerLastName in the source schema out to (and attaching to) the String Concatenate functoid in the center pane.

5. Click and drag the functoid over to the CustomerName element on the destination schema, attaching it and completing the source to destination path. Your map should look similar to Figure 7-20.

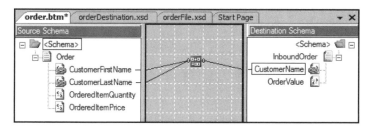

Figure 7-20. *The current functoid attachments*

6. Right-click the functoid in the center pane and select Configure Functoid Inputs to view its parameters, as shown in Figure 7-21. Notice that BizTalk will concatenate the fields in the order in which they are attached to the functoid.

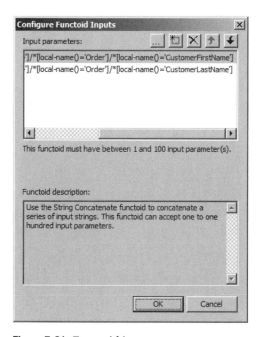

Figure 7-21. *Functoid inputs*

7. If you look closely at the parameters, you may notice a problem. When the concatenation takes place, the output will literally be strung together. So concatenating Joe and Smith will output as JoeSmith. You need to add a space character to the mix, and you do that by adding another parameter in the Configure Functoid Inputs dialog box. At the top of the Configure Functoid Inputs dialog box, click the button with an ellipsis (its tooltip says "Insert new parameter"). An empty row is added to the list of parameters.

8. Add the space character as the value, as shown in Figure 7-22. You may need to double-click the icon to the left before you can enter a value in the text box. Then click OK.

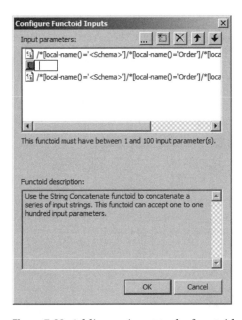

Figure 7-22. *Adding an input to the functoid*

The string concatenation mapping process is complete.

Using the Multiplication Functoid

Let's now turn our attention to the math that needs to be done for the quantity and price elements.

1. In the Mapper toolbox, click the Mathematical Functoids node and locate the Multiplication functoid, as shown in Figure 7-23.

2. Click and drag the functoid out to the gridded center pane of the Mapper.

3. Click and drag OrderedItemQuantity out to the new functoid.

4. Click and drag OrderedItemPrice out to the new functoid.

5. Click and drag the functoid over to the destination schema's OrderValue element.

And that's it! Your map is complete, as shown in Figure 7-24.

Figure 7-23. *Locating the Multiplication functoid*

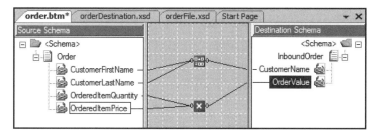

Figure 7-24. *The complete map with functoids*

Testing the Map with Functoids

Before testing the map, you need to add the input instance file for the test, as you did in the previous example. Then you can see how your functoids worked.

1. Right-click the map file in the Solution Explorer and select Properties.

2. Add orderFile.xml as the TestMap Input Instance, as shown in Figure 7-25. Click OK to continue.

3. Right-click the map file name and select Test Map.

4. In the results listing, Ctrl-click to follow the link to the output XML file.

As you can see in Figure 7-26, your map has successfully concatenated the customer name as well as applied the multiplication process to the quantity and price elements. You have to admit, that's pretty cool!

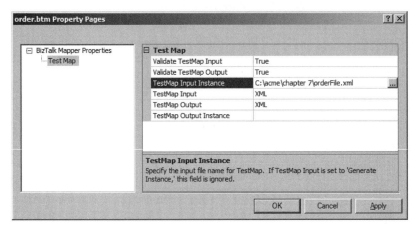

Figure 7-25. *Adding the orderFile.xml for testing*

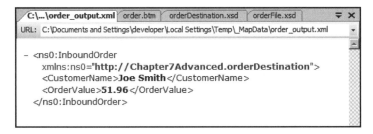

Figure 7-26. *The test results*

Summary

In this chapter, you created a few maps and implemented a pair of functoids as we began our exploration of the BizTalk schema abilities. The BizTalk Mapper is an intuitive interface to work with and allows you to create message-conversion maps in a relatively short amount of time. As cool as the mapping utility is, it is just one of the many tools that BizTalk delivers. As you progress through the book, you'll discover and use more of the BizTalk product power!

■ ■ ■

CHAPTER 8

Ports

So far, we've discussed messages and their proprietary structure. You've seen how you can shape and mold a variety of data formats into content that is meaningful to your organization. But simply having a message available does little for your enterprise. You need to get that data into your system in a safe and efficient manner. That's where BizTalk ports come in. Ports allow the BizTalk environment to receive and send those messages that you've worked with so diligently.

Within the BizTalk port structure are four basic entities: receive ports, receive locations, send ports, and send port groups. If you open the BizTalk Administration Console, you will see folders for each of these components. They're empty for now, but you'll change that over the course of this chapter.

At this point, you need to understand how the four port components fit into the overall concept of moving data from an external resource to your BizTalk message box. In this chapter, you'll get an overview of the receive port and send port structure. Then you'll see how these ports work in a sample application.

What Are BizTalk Ports?

In the previous chapters, you've taken the first steps toward creating a full-scale messaging application by understanding and building sample messages. Getting those messages into the BizTalk machine is the next logical step to take. So let's assume that your vendor, Acme Inc., has provided you with a list of product pricing that you need to adopt in your retail system for evaluation. The file is XML:

```
<nsO:Products xmlns:nsO="http://acme.com/ports/products">
  <Product>
    <ProductID>10001</ProductID>
    <ProductName>Acme warp drive components</ProductName>
    <Price>123.56</Price>
    <Quantity>2</Quantity>
  </Product>
  <Product>
    <ProductID>10013</ProductID>
    <ProductName>Acme cloaking device</ProductName>
    <Price>234.99</Price>
    <Quantity>1</Quantity>
  </Product>
```

```
<Product>
  <ProductID>10021</ProductID>
  <ProductName>Acme Time Travel Device</ProductName>
  <Price>855.99</Price>
  <Quantity>9</Quantity>
</Product>
<Product>
  <ProductID>10045</ProductID>
  <ProductName>Acme Personal Clone</ProductName>
  <Price>900.99</Price>
  <Quantity>1</Quantity>
</Product>
</ns0:Order>
```

The vendor has saved the file as acmeProducts.xml and will make the list available to your organization on a daily basis. For you to really do anything worthwhile within BizTalk, you need to get that information into your system for processing. Figure 8-1 shows a basic premise for this reception path.

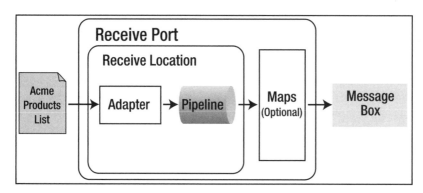

Figure 8-1. *Receive port structure*

The Receive Port Structure

As you can see in Figure 8-1, you have a receive port and a receive location. So what exactly is the difference? A *port* is a "logical" container for the "physical" *receive location*.

Imagine that you're sailing to Paradise Island on your brand-new boat, for a well-deserved vacation. You're going to be pulling into Paradise Island International Port and docking at Pier 13. The international port of arrival is your receive port, and the pier is a receive location. Is it possible that your port could be made up of many piers? Yes, it's highly probable that there are multiple locations for other vacationers to dock their boats. And such is the case with BizTalk ports. Ultimately, this becomes excruciatingly important when you design and implement your routing structure.

A port is essentially a container of locations where you can obtain data. A receive port could be made up of as many locations as you want—limited by your system resources, of course.

So within your port, you'll be constructing a location. This will represent your physical "intake" of data. As you can see in Figure 8-1, the location, much like the port, is composed of components: receive adapters and receive pipelines.

Receive Adapters

BizTalk Server ships with a few "stock" adapters that you can use:

- File

- FTP

- HTTP

- MQSeries

- MSMQ

- POP3

- SOAP

- SQL

- SharePoint Services

As you can see from this list, it is somewhat obvious what an adapter might do: It provides a communication method for a particular transfer method. So if you have a vendor that provides files via FTP, you have an adapter that is uniquely suited to that form of transaction.

You'll be using the File adapter as the conduit of choice for this chapter's sample application. This will allow you to "physically" connect your BizTalk message box to an actual folder location on the hard drive.

Pipelines

We'll be covering pipelines in detail in the next chapter, but for now, you should at least understand the basic premise of the component. After leaving the adapter stage, your message will enter into the pipeline. As its name would suggest, a *pipeline* essentially "tunnels" your data from one point to another. During that transition, you're given the opportunity to process the message with various BizTalk components. The BizTalk installation process provides two stock receive pipelines right out of the gate:

- The PassThruReceive pipeline does not make any modifications to the message.

- The XMLReceive pipeline parses the XML message.

Fortunately, those aren't the only pipelines available to the BizTalk developer. As you'll learn in Chapter 9, it's quite possible to build a custom pipeline to accomplish your own message processing. You'll see how the individual pipeline is actually a collection of unique stages, depending on the port direction. Figure 8-2 shows the stages of the receive pipeline.

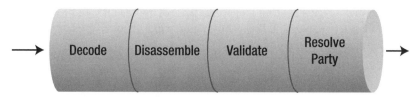

Figure 8-2. *Four phases of the receive pipeline*

The send pipeline is composed of three phases, as shown in Figure 8-3.

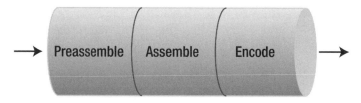

Figure 8-3. *The three phases of the send pipeline*

That's all you need to know about pipelines for this chapter.

Maps

In Chapter 6, you had the chance to work with the BizTalk Mapper. Building a map allows you to take a foreign message schema and create an XSLT transformation process to match the internal schemas that your corporate processes demand. It is during this phase of the reception that you may assign your own customized maps. I say "may," because the presence of a BizTalk map at this point is completely optional. If your port does not make use of the transformational powers of mapping, it simply continues on to the final destination: the BizTalk message box.

One popular implementation of maps, in general, is the process of mapping on the receive and send ports. This is an incredibly fast process and eliminates the need to involve a costly orchestration instantiation, as the messages are mapped as they are moved from point to point.

The Send Port Structure

One of the key concepts that I feel most people miss when attempting to understand the send port process is that the ports are built on a subscription model of implementation. I explained subscription in Chapter 5, but when it comes to constructing send ports, it becomes plainly evident that the concept is an important one. Without it, your send points would be unresponsive and pointless.

The easiest way to understand the structure of the send port and how it relates to the receive port is to take Figure 8-1 and flip it over, as shown in Figure 8-4.

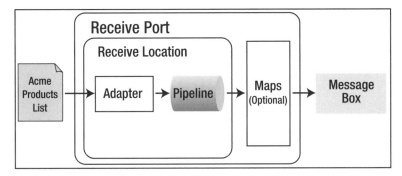

Figure 8-4. *Receive port flipped*

Okay, so maybe that wasn't as funny as I had hoped, but it does get us one step closer to the truth. Figure 8-5 depicts the actual send port process.

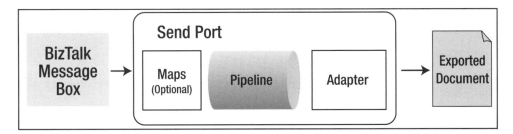

Figure 8-5. *The send port structure*

Wait a minute! What happened to the location block? One of the variations of the send port is that it isn't necessarily tied to a particular location, as it is more interested in subscribing to what the BizTalk message box contains. For receive ports, it is necessary for locations to exist, because it is quite possible that you'll have a multitude of location points for any given reception area.

But what if you want to send out multiple messages, based on a single message process? For instance, let's say that your BizTalk system receives the XML product pricing file from Acme Inc. on a daily basis. You process the inbound message, send it to the message box, and consequently, you would like to export the same pricing file to various department systems for further processing:

- To the Replenishment department, to update the quantity on hand

- To the store location, to update shelf tags

- To the Accounting department, for financial updates

That's where *send port groups* come in. Groups allow you to take a single, outbound message and send it to multiple ports. One port may be a file drop, another a SQL database update, and a third may be a call to a web service. All of those would involve creating separate send port entities within the same send port group, as shown in Figure 8-6.

Note You won't be creating send port groups for the examples in this book, but I encourage you to follow up with *Pro BizTalk Server 2006* (Apress, ISBN: 1-59059-699-4) when you're ready to try them out.

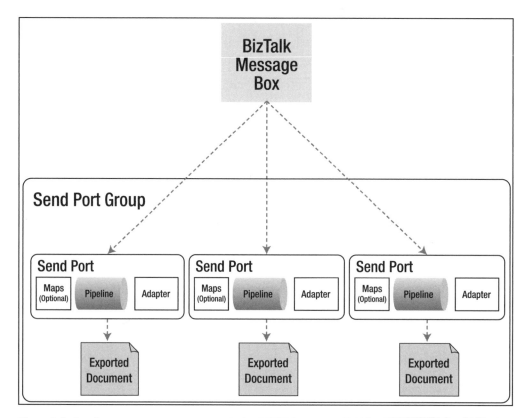

Figure 8-6. *Send port groups*

Building the Import/Export Application

Now that you understand the basic port concepts, you're ready for an example. But before we start our sample application, let's discuss what you hope to accomplish. Your vendor, Acme Inc., has provided you the aforementioned XML products file. You'll create an input directory, from which you'll draw the file into the BizTalk system, and an export directory, where you will place the new file after running it through BizTalk processes. You won't actually perform any kind of actions against the file, aside from simply acquiring it into the BizTalk message box and dumping it back into the output directory. To obtain this result, you'll need to build receive and send ports. The path the file will travel is illustrated in Figure 8-7.

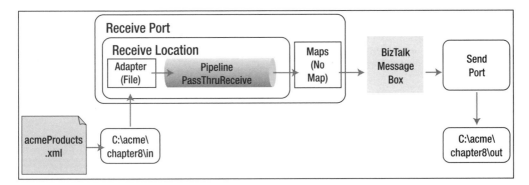

Figure 8-7. *Import/export application path*

Creating Physical File Directories

One of the primary requirements that the application will have is a physical hard drive location where you can drop your XML file and a corresponding directory where BizTalk can place the output.

Also, you'll need to modify a security setting that seems to be a global "gotcha." If the BizTalk service does not have read/write access to the folders you create for your application, the application won't pick up or deliver the XML files located in those folders.

Follow these steps to get started:

1. Create a directory named `c:\acme\chapter8\in`.

2. Create another directory named `c:\acme\chapter8\out`.

3. Start Windows Explorer.

4. Find the `acme` directory, right-click the directory name, and select Sharing and Security.

5. Select the Security tab in the Properties dialog box.

6. Click the Add button.

7. Click the Advanced button.

8. Click the Find Now button.

9. Find and select the BizTalk Service user account. Click OK.

10. Click OK again to return to the Properties dialog box.

11. Give the BizTalk service full control access to the folder. Click OK.

Your BizTalk application now has full access to the file structure.

■**Caution** Any file that is set to read-only will not be picked up by the application. If you're like me, it will take a few of these "gotchas" before you set directory security correctly every time.

Building the Receive Port

So now that you have a general understanding of what the port will do, let's go ahead and create a simple receive port to accept the acmeProducts.xml file.

1. Open the BizTalk Server 2006 Administration Console.

2. Right-click Applications and select New ➤ Application, as shown in Figure 8-8.

Figure 8-8. *Creating a new BizTalk application*

3. Name your application chapter8, and then click OK.

4. Expand the chapter8 directory.

5. Right-click Receive Ports and select New ➤ One-Way Receive Port, as shown in Figure 8-9.

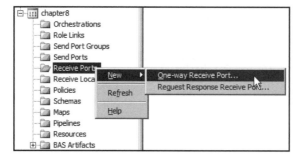

Figure 8-9. *Adding the receive port*

After adding the receive port, you'll need to specify receive location, adapter, and pipeline information. You'll do that from the Properties dialog box, shown in Figure 8-10, which appeared after you chose to add the port.

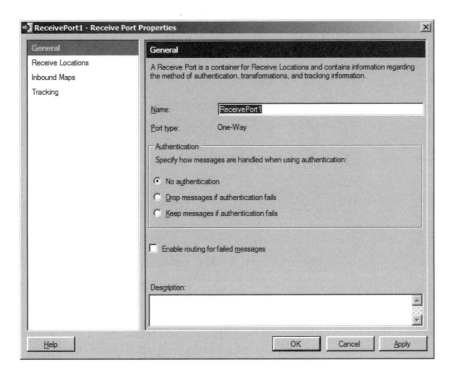

Figure 8-10. *Receive Port Properties dialog box*

Adding the Receive Location

Now you will add a new receive location and choose the adapter and pipeline. As mentioned earlier, you'll be using the File adapter for this particular application. To take advantage of the unique abilities that the adapter has, you'll need to point it to the correct hard drive location. You will then need to configure the File adapter, so that it has an idea where to locate your XML file. As you'll recall, you created an in and out directory for processing the files for this application.

1. In the General section of the Receive Port Properties dialog box, leave the Name property at its default setting (you'll be using that again later). Click the Receive Locations selection in the left pane.

2. Click the New button in the right pane to add a new location. Another Properties dialog box will open, as shown in Figure 8-11. This is where you'll add the physical attributes to your file's location. The Receive Location Properties dialog box provides easy access to the adapter (Transport), as well as the pipeline.

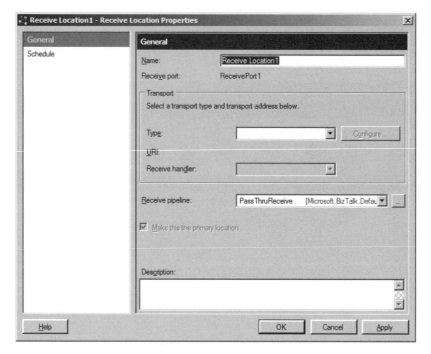

Figure 8-11. *Receive Location Properties dialog box*

3. Select FILE from the Transport Type drop-down list, as shown in Figure 8-12. After selecting the File adapter, you'll notice that Receive Pipeline option has been automatically set as PassThruReceive. Coincidentally, that's the value you want.

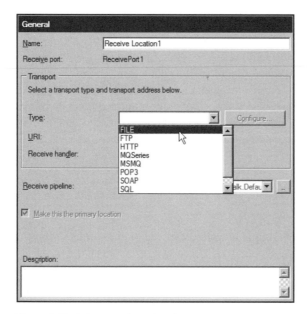

Figure 8-12. *Selecting the File adapter*

4. Click the Configure button so that you can point to the appropriate directory.

5. In the FILE Transport Properties dialog box, click the Browse button and locate the in directory you created earlier. Your dialog box should now appear as shown in Figure 8-13.

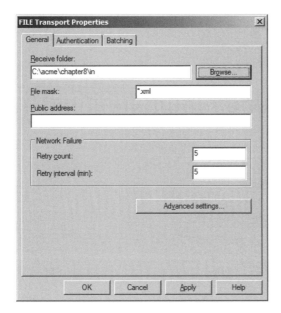

Figure 8-13. *File transport specifications*

6. The File Mask setting, *.xml, is exactly what you're after, so there is no need to modify that. You're not interested in any of the other settings for this component, so click OK.

7. Click OK to accept the settings in the Receive Location Properties dialog box.

8. You won't be assigning a map to the inbound process, so go ahead and click OK in the Receive Port Properties dialog box.

Enabling the Receive Location

Now that you've set up the receive port, let's enable it.

1. Click the Receive Ports selection in the left pane of the Administration Console to verify that ReceivePort1 does indeed exist.

2. Select Receive Locations. You'll notice that the location is Disabled, as shown in Figure 8-14.

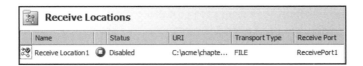

Figure 8-14. *Receive location at a standstill*

3. Right-click ReceiveLocation1 and select Enable. The red (stopped) symbol will change to a green arrow, indicating that the location is now alive and well, waiting diligently for any XML file to drop by.

With your receive location up and running, your port is now configured and ready for action. However, if you tried to test the application now, you would only create a suspended message. Before you can push the acmeProducts.xml file through the BizTalk system, you need to create the send port.

Creating the Send Port

For the sample application, you will be adding a single send port, tied to a File adapter.

1. In the Administration Console, right-click the Send Ports folder and select New ➤ Static One-Way Send Port, as shown in Figure 8-15.

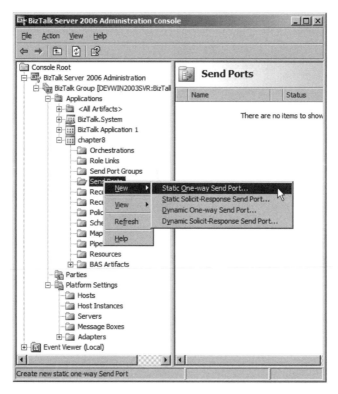

Figure 8-15. *Adding a send port*

2. In the Send Port Properties dialog box, accept SendPort1 as the default port name. Select FILE from the Transport Type drop-down list. Keep the default PassThruTransmit pipeline. You're using the PassThruTransmit pipeline here because you're not interested in performing any preshipment processing for this particular application. Your Send Port Properties dialog box should look like Figure 8-16.

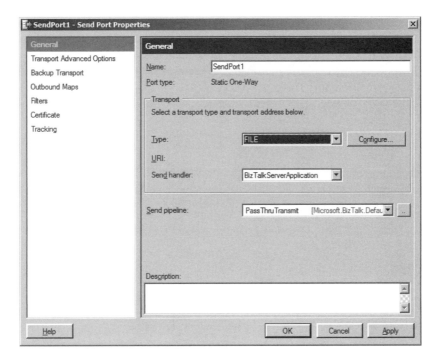

Figure 8-16. *Send Port Properties dialog box*

3. Click the Configure button.

4. Click the Browse button to find and select the out directory that you created earlier, as shown in Figure 8-17. The out location is where the send port will send the processed message.

Figure 8-17. *Selecting the outbound file location*

5. Your FILE Transport Properties dialog box should now look like Figure 8-18. One interesting point to note here is the File Name setting. When the file output is generated by BizTalk, a unique `MessageID` will be generated and declared as the name for the outbound XML file. You're free to modify this as required by the application requirements for your destination port. For now, just accept this default naming scheme. Click OK to close the FILE Transport Properties dialog box.

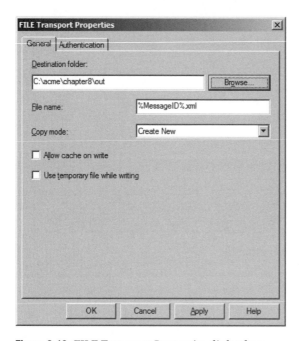

Figure 8-18. *FILE Transport Properties dialog box*

6. Back in the Send Port Properties dialog box, in the left pane, select Filters, to assign a filter to the port. As I stated earlier, send ports are built on the subscription concept. Your port spends its time looking at the BizTalk message box, but if you don't give it something specific to monitor, it will never retrieve the message from the engine, and the processed message will remain in the box forever, unprocessable.

7. In the right pane of the dialog box is the Filters panel, with an empty row for entering your own filter expressions. Under Property, find and select `BTS.ReceivePortName`. Under Value, enter the name that you assigned to your receive port. (Remember when I said that you would be using the receive port name later?) Enter `ReceivePort1` for the value, provided that you accepted the default name as recommended. Your Filters panel should appear as shown in Figure 8-19.

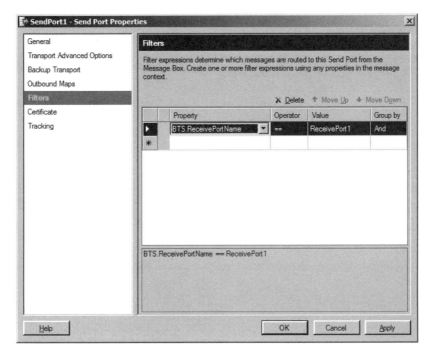

Figure 8-19. *Filter subscription statement*

8. Click OK to exit the Send Port Properties dialog box.

9. Click Send Ports in the left pane of the Administration Console. You'll see that the port has a red/stopped status, as shown in Figure 8-20. "Unenlisted" simply means that the port has yet to be "enlisted" to a particular message box subscription. Yes, you did in fact create a subscription filter in the Properties dialog box, but you need to turn on (or *enlist*) the subscription for the port to function correctly.

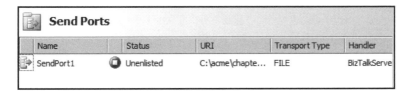

Figure 8-20. *The send port is unenlisted.*

10. Right-click the status and select Start, as shown in Figure 8-21. The Status column should show green/started, indicating that the send port is now observing the BizTalk message box and will promptly withdraw any message with a receive port name context of ReceivePort1.

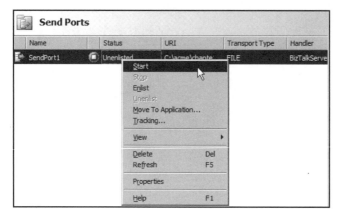

Figure 8-21. *Starting the send port enlistment*

And that completes your receive port and send port for this application. Let's see how it works.

Testing the Application

It's time to test the application by dropping an XML file into your input directory.

1. Create the acmeProducts.xml file based on the data given earlier in the chapter.

2. Copy the file into the input directory. After a moment, the file will disappear, as it is drawn into the BizTalk system. It will consequently be passed back out into the out directory, as shown in Figure 8-22.

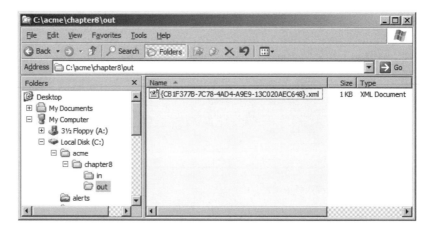

Figure 8-22. *The port pass-through process at work*

Notice that the file has been renamed, taking on the MessageID value, as anticipated. If you open the file, you'll find that it has the same XML information as the original file. That's to be expected, since you didn't perform any actions on it from within the BizTalk environment, aside from passing it along the line from the receive port to the send port.

Summary

The file transport is only one of the many adapters that ship with BizTalk. I encourage you to follow up this chapter with an in-depth discovery of the others, which you may find you'll want to use in your own enterprise applications.

In this chapter, you learned how to create and implement the receive and send ports for your BizTalk environment. You took a cursory look at a few of the components that make up the port system. In the next chapter, we'll spend a little more time with one of those components: pipelines.

CHAPTER 9

■■■

Pipelines

Years ago, I was able to spend a few years in Fairbanks, Alaska. One of my most memorable moments was the time I spent walking along a minor section of the Trans-Alaskan pipeline. Undoubtedly, you're asking "What is so impressive about a steel tube full of oil?" Well the "steel tube" runs for nearly 800 miles through some of the most desolate and inhabitable terrain on this planet. It is capable of enduring earthquakes and has done so on numerous occasions.

The pipeline runs from Prudhoe Bay (the northern most portion of Alaska) down to the port of Valdez and has one of the most intricate support networks for simply being a "steel tube full of oil." Contrary to popular belief, the pipeline does not run uninterrupted for the 800 miles it must travel. Along the way are 11 pumping stations, each with 4 electric pumps that work to maintain the dynamic pressure needed for the fluid to arrive in Valdez.

Another interesting addition to the process is the implementation of radiator-like cooling components attached to various portions of the tube. When the oil emerges from the earth's surface, it does so at a toasty 180 degrees. If allowed to run at this temperature, structural devices would, themselves, become quite warm and melt the frozen tundra surrounding the pipeline. Eventually, the pipeline would begin to sink and inevitably, damage to the pipeline would ensue. So the pipeline is much more than a steel tube. The same could be said of BizTalk pipelines.

BizTalk pipelines have much more functionality than simply moving data from the adapter to the message box. BizTalk allows you to perform a variety of manipulative processes on the data as it makes it way through the server system.

In this chapter, you will work through a sample application that demonstrates what pipelines can do. But before you jump in and build that application, you need to have a full understanding of what the pipeline is and how you can use it in a message environment.

Pipeline Basics

At their core, pipelines are responsible for moving messages to and from the BizTalk message box, as shown in Figure 9-1.

Figure 9-1. *A few of the components in the messaging process*

In Chapter 8, you saw that you can implement pipelines in two directional locations: receive locations and send ports. Each is composed of multiple stages, within which you have the chance to modify the messages being delivered in either direction.

A key selling point for BizTalk Server is the idea that you can throw just about any data format into the mix, and a savvy developer will be able to design an acceptable method of processing for the inbound file. As we've discussed previously, all messages coming into the system need to be translated into an internal XML format. The beauty of BizTalk is that we're able to accomplish that without a ton of coding. The individual stages allow distinct modifications to the incoming or outgoing messages.

Receive Pipeline Stages

Four stages form a complete receive pipeline:

Decode: This stage takes in an encrypted message and outputs plain text, for processing. For example, S/MIME decoding would take place during the Decode stage.

Disassemble: On occasion, messages may be "packaged," as is the case with the sample application for this chapter. You will have a CSV file with a list of products wrapped into one file, and you will need to have this product disassembled into individual product files. The Disassemble stage will provide a flat file disassembler that will parse the incoming file and prepare it for delivery to the BizTalk message box as individual XML units.

Validate: It may be in your best interest to validate those disassembled messages (or any message for that matter), and you'll perform that action in the Validate stage. Any validating components that you have will be run against every message in the process and in this process only.

Resolve Party: The last stage in the pipeline accomplishes a single, basic task: populating the SourcePartyID property based on the original sender of the message passing through the pipeline. The property is populated based on the ability of BizTalk to validate the sending certificate or security identifier (SID).

Each of these individual components has a unique set of toolbox options associated with it. If the stock tools are not sufficient for your application, you can create .NET or COM components that can be implemented via the pipeline stages, for both receive and send pipelines. Figure 9-2 demonstrates the relationship between the receive pipeline stages and the representation within Visual Studio.

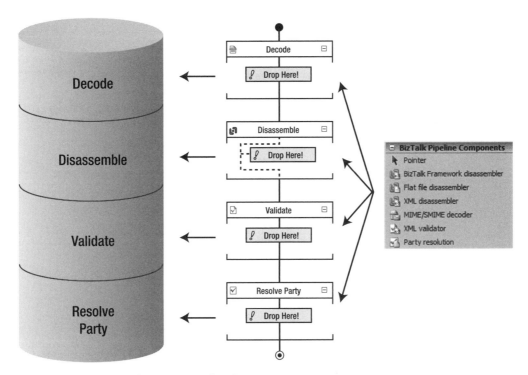

Figure 9-2. *Receive pipeline stages and tools*

Send Pipeline Stages

A send pipeline has only three stages in which to prepare the outbound message:

Preassemble: This stage prepares messages for the outbound process. If necessary, you can add customized code for this processing.

Assemble: When BizTalk has finished processing your message, it will be outbound in XML format. However, you might not want the XML as your desired output. You could pack the data into a flat file for shipment to other business entities.

Encode: As you would expect, you would encode your outbound message within this stage. In much the same way that you might decode S/MIME on the receive pipeline, you could encrypt with S/MIME as needed.

As for the receive pipeline stages, BizTalk provides a set of tools for working with the send pipeline stages, as shown in Figure 9-3. You'll notice that there aren't any stock toolbox components that will operate within the Preassemble stage.

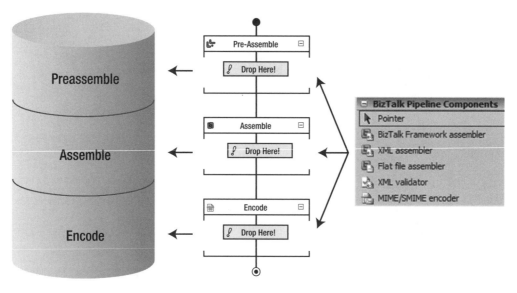

Figure 9-3. *Send pipeline stages and tools*

As interesting as these individual stages may be, it is far easier to comprehend the overall process when you put the components to work.

Building the Sample Pipeline Application

In this chapter's example, you will create a CSV file, parse it with your receive pipeline, and push it out as four individual CSV files. You will be using the flat file disassembler and assembler as you build the receive and send pipelines. Figure 9-4 illustrates the path that your file will take as it is being processed within the BizTalk environment.

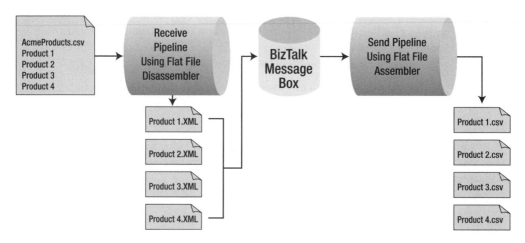

Figure 9-4. *Sample application path*

You'll begin by creating a schema project. You'll create the necessary flat file schema that will help to parse your .csv file. After a successful build, you'll add a second project to the solution and build the appropriate pipelines.

Creating the Schema Project

Let's first build the .csv file. Open a text editor (like WordPad) and create the following document, pressing Enter at the end of each line:

```
10001, Acme warp drive components, 123.56, 2
10013, Acme cloaking device, 234.99, 1
10021, Acme Time Travel Device, 855.99, 9
10045, Acme Personal Clone, 900.99, 1
```

Save the file as AcmeProducts.csv at C:\acme\chapter9.

You could probably guess the schema, or at least come close: ProductID, ProductName, ProductPrice, and ProductQuantity. You'll be using these values as you create your flat file schema. Typically, you would want to use the Flat File Schema Wizard, as you did in Chapter 6, as it is a powerful and fast tool. However, here you will build your schema by hand, so that you understand what is involved behind the scenes when you're working with flat files.

1. Start Visual Studio 2005.

2. Select File ➤ New ➤ Project. Select Empty BizTalk Project, name it AcmeSchemas, and save it at C:\acme\chapter9. Change the solution name to Chapter9. Then click OK.

3. Right-click the project name in the Solution Explorer and select Add ➤ New Item ➤ Flat File Schema.

4. Save your schema as AcmeFlatFileSchema.xsd, and then click Add. After the file has loaded, you should see the XML representation of the schema.

5. Right-click the Root node and rename it to Products.

6. Right-click Products and choose Add a Child Record. Name the new record Product.

7. Right-click the Product node and add a Child Field Element, naming it ProductID.

8. Repeat step 7 to add three more fields under the Product node: ProductName, ProductPrice, and ProductQuantity. Your schema should appear as shown in Figure 9-5.

Figure 9-5. *The modified Products schema*

Setting Node Properties

Because you are going to parse a flat file, you must dictate the delimiters that will be used by the schema when searching through the CSV file.

1. Highlight the Products node, right-click, and select Properties to bring up the Properties window for the node.

2. Set the Child Delimiter Type to hexadecimal.

3. Set the Child Delimiter property to 0x0D 0x0A. This is the hexadecimal representation of a document line feed.

4. Set the Child Order property to be Postfix. We'll be parsing the "rows" after the passing of each child record.

■**Note** Notice that you have a few options for the Child Order property: Postfix, Infix, and Prefix. With Postfix, the delimiter appears after the data that is being delimited (*field,field,field,*). With Prefix, the delimiter appears before the data that you're deliminating (*,field,field,field*). With Infix, the delimiter appears between items of data (*field, field, field*).

---

5. Select the Product node, right-click, and select Properties to open the Properties window for that node.

6. Set the Child Delimiter Type to Character.

7. Add , (a comma) to the Child Delimiter property.

8. Set the Child Order property to Infix. You'll be parsing each of the product details with the comma as an inline process, so Infix is the appropriate choice.

9. Save the schema.

You're almost finished with the schema project, but you need to modify the project properties before you deploy it.

Modifying the Schema Project Properties

First and foremost, you need to create a strong name key file that you'll add to both projects (the schema project and the pipeline project that you'll create next).

1. Open the Visual Studio 2005 Command Prompt utility (Start ➤ Programs ➤ Microsoft Visual Studio 2005 ➤ Visual Studio 2005 ➤ Visual Studio 2005 Command Prompt).

2. Drill down into your working directory at C:\acme\chapter9 and create a strong name key file by entering the following into the Command Prompt window:

```
sn -k acmeKeyfile.snk
```

After a moment, a key file will be added to your working directory.

3. To add the key to the schema project, right-click the project name and select Properties.

4. Select Assembly under Common Properties.

5. On the right side of the Property Pages dialog box, locate Assembly Key File. Find and add the key file that you created in step 2.

6. Expand the Configuration Properties node on the left side.

7. Change the application name to Chapter9Pipelines, as shown in Figure 9-6.

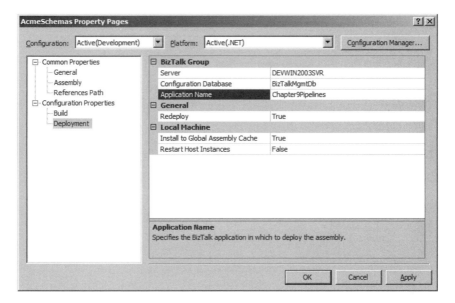

Figure 9-6. *Modifying the schema project properties*

8. Click OK to save the settings and close the dialog box.

Building and Deploying the Schema Project

Your schema project is ready for action!

1. Right-click the project and select Build.

2. When the build is complete, right-click again and select Deploy.

The application should deploy without any problems.

Creating the Pipeline Project

Now that you have a flat file schema in place, you're ready to build the project with customized pipelines.

1. In Visual Studio, select File ➤ Add ➤ New Project.

2. Select Empty BizTalk Project and name it AcmePipelines. Be sure to add it to the current solution.

Adding the Receive Pipeline

You will now add the receive pipeline as a flat file disassembler, assign the document schema of the assembler, and then configure it to parse the incoming file correctly.

1. Right-click the AcmePipelines project name in the Solution Explorer and select Add ➤ New Item.

2. Select Receive Pipeline and save it as AcmeFlatFileReceivePipeline.btb.

3. After the pipeline has loaded into the design environment, drag a Flat File Disassembler component from the toolbox out to the pipeline and drop it into the Disassemble stage, as shown in Figure 9-7.

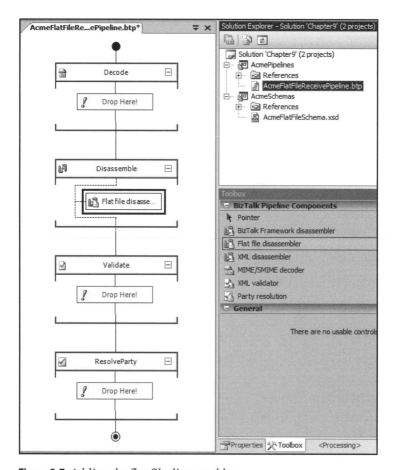

Figure 9-7. *Adding the flat file disassembler*

4. To add the reference to the `AcmeFlatFileSchema`, right-click the pipeline project name and select Add Reference. Switch to the Projects tab and add the `AcmeSchemas` reference by clicking the Add button. Click OK after the reference has been added to the list.

5. Highlight the flat file object on the receive pipeline and open the Properties window. Click the Document Schema drop-down list and select `AcmeSchemas.AcmeFlatFileSchema`, as shown in Figure 9-8.

Figure 9-8. *Adding the schemas reference*

Your receive pipeline is complete and ready for action. Let's shift our attention to the send pipeline.

Adding the Send Pipeline

You will add the send pipeline as a flat file assembler.

1. Right-click the pipelines project name and select Add ➤ New Item.

2. Select Send Pipeline and save it as `AcmeFlatFileSendPipeline.btp`.

3. Drag a Flat File Assembler component from the toolbox out to the Assemble stage, as shown in Figure 9-9.

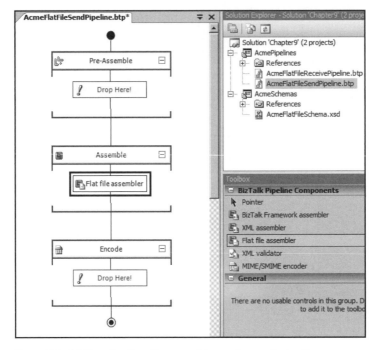

Figure 9-9. *Adding the flat file assembler to the send pipeline*

4. Highlight the Flat File Assembler component and open its Properties window.

5. Click the drop-down list for the Document Schema property and select
   AcmeSchemas.AcmeFlatFileSchema, as you did for the receive pipeline.

Modifying the Pipeline Project Properties

Before deploying the project, you need to set a few project configurations, similar to the
process you performed with AcmeSchemas.

1. Right-click the pipelines project and select Properties.

2. Select the Assembly node on the left.

3. Find the same key file that you used with the AcmeSchemas project, and add it to the
   AssemblyKeyFile, as shown in Figure 9-10.

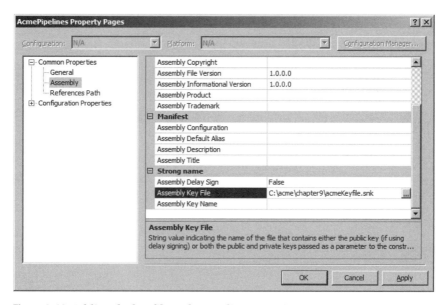

Figure 9-10. *Adding the key file to the pipeline project*

4. Expand the Configuration Properties node.

5. Select the Deployment node.

6. Set the application name to the same value used with `AcmeSchemas`: `Chapter9Pipelines`.

Your deployment configuration should be similar to that shown in Figure 9-11.

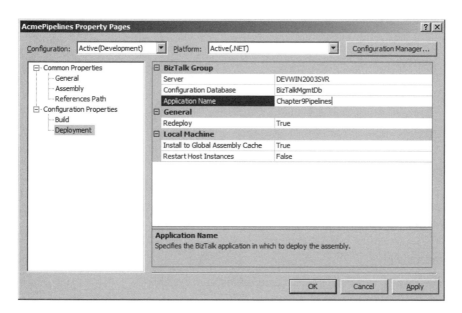

Figure 9-11. *Pipeline project deployment configuration*

Building and Deploying the Pipeline Project

You're now ready to build and deploy your pipeline project.

1. Right-click the AcmePipelines project and select Build.

2. After a successful build, right-click AcmePipelines again and select Deploy.

The application is now deployed to BizTalk Server.

Testing the Pipelines Project

You'll use the BizTalk Administration Console to verify the deployment and to create the necessary components for testing.

1. Start the BizTalk Server Administration Console.

2. Expand the Console Root node until you find your application (Chapter9Pipelines). You should be able to find your schema as well as the pipelines, as shown in Figure 9-12.

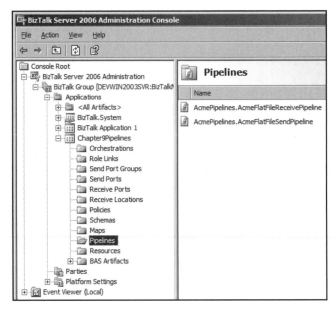

Figure 9-12. *Your pipelines at the ready*

Before you can test the application, you need to create the appropriate receive port and location and a corresponding send port.

Creating the Receive Port

You'll create a simple receive port to accept the AcmeProducts.csv file.

1. Right-click Receive Ports and select New ➤ One-way Receive Port.

2. Accept the default name of ReceivePort1 and select the Receive Locations node to the left.

3. Click the New button in the panel to the right.

4. Accept `Receive Location 1` as the name for the location.

5. Click the drop-down list for Transport Type and select FILE.

6. Click the Configure button.

7. Click Browse for the Receive Folder location and add a new folder named `In` to the `Chapter9` root folder. Click OK to accept the `In` folder location.

8. Modify the File Mask property to accept only `*.csv` files. Your FILE Transport Properties dialog box should look like Figure 9-13. Click OK to close the dialog box.

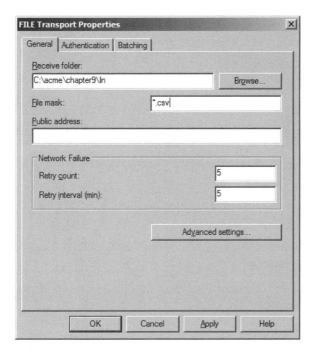

Figure 9-13. *File transport properties*

9. Back in the Receive Location1 Properties dialog box, click the drop-down list for the Receive Pipeline and select your custom `AcmeFlatFileReceivePipeline`. Your dialog box should look like Figure 9-14. Click OK.

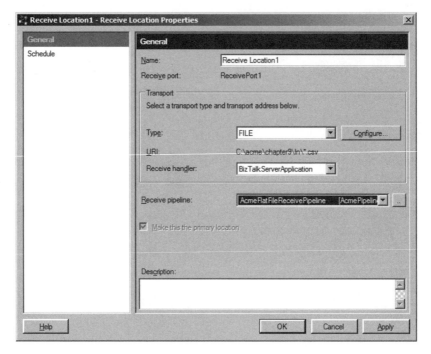

Figure 9-14. *Receive location properties*

10. You don't need to modify the receive port properties any further, so click OK to close the dialog box.

11. Highlight the Receive Locations node in the Administration Console. You should see your new location, stopped by default.

12. Right-click the location and select Enable. Your location should be green-lit and ready for action, as shown in Figure 9-15.

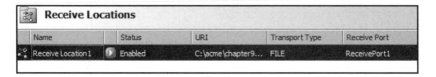

Figure 9-15. *Receive location at attention*

Creating the Send Port

You need to create a send port that the BizTalk messaging system can use for output. Other-wise, your documents would reside forever in the depths of the message box.

1. Right-click the Send Ports node and select Add ➤ Static One-way Send Port.

2. Again, select FILE for Transport Type and click the Configure button.

3. In the FILE Transport Properties dialog box, click the Browse button for the Destination Folder option and create a new folder on the `Chapter9` root, naming it `Out`. Modify the File Name property to output a `.csv` file rather than an `.xml` file. Your dialog box should look like Figure 9-16. Click OK.

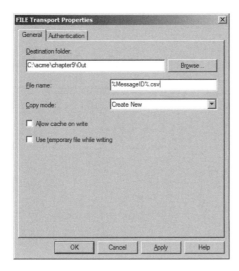

Figure 9-16. *Sending transport properties*

4. In the Send Port Properties dialog box, click the drop-down list next to Send Pipeline and select your custom `AcmeFlatFileSendPipeline`.

5. Select the Filters node in the left panel of the Send Port Properties dialog box.

6. Modify the send port so that it subscribes to the receive port. On the Filters panel, add the subscription expression so that the port is monitoring for the context of `BTS.ReceivePortName = = ReceivePort1`, as shown in Figure 9-17.

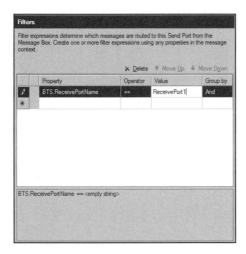

Figure 9-17. *Adding the filter expression*

7. Click the General node and verify that your send port settings look like those shown in Figure 9-18. Then click OK.

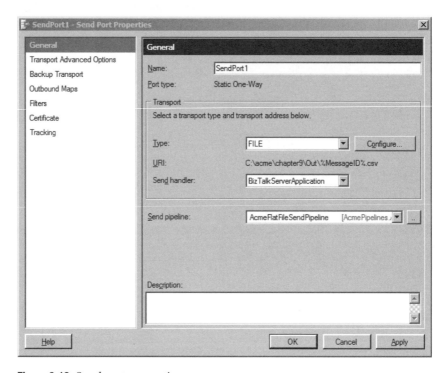

Figure 9-18. *Send port properties*

8. Back in the BizTalk Administration Console, the send port should now be visible and stopped. Right-click the send port and select Start.

Your application is now ready for testing!

Running the Application

Let's see the pipelines in action.

1. Set the folder permissions to allow the BizTalk service full control of the Chapter9 root. (You performed this same operation in Chapter 8, if you need to revisit the steps.)

2. Find the acmeProducts.csv file that you created at the start of the example and drop a copy into the In directory. After a moment, your file will disappear, having been pulled into the BizTalk messaging system.

3. Switch over to the Out directory. You should find four separate files, as shown in Figure 9-19.

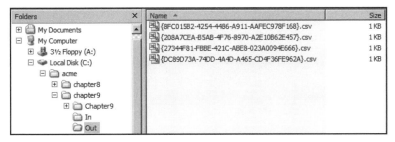

Figure 9-19. *The .csv files created by the application*

If you open one of the .csv files, you will find that it has been parsed by the BizTalk messaging system into individual product files. Figure 9-20 shows an opened product file from the collection of four.

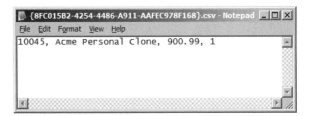

Figure 9-20. *The parsed product file*

Summary

In this chapter, you implemented both the receive and send pipelines in a sample application. You were able to take advantage of the flat file disassembler, using the AcmeFlatFileSchema as the base unit of transformation.

As I mentioned earlier, the stock pipeline components are not the end-all for production manipulation of data. As you progress with BizTalk, you'll be able to write your own tasks composed of .NET code or COM components. You'll find that the pipeline can be as simple or as powerful as you would like it to be. You'll definitely want to check out *Pro BizTalk Server 2006* (Apress, ISBN: 1-59059-699-4) for further study on the custom pipeline building process.

In the next chapter, we'll cover the next step in message processing: the orchestration. Within the realm of orchestrations, you can attend to data in ways that pipelines simply can't. You'll build and deploy yet another sample application, which should help to further demystify the "magic" of BizTalk Server 2006.

CHAPTER 10

Orchestrations

When you think of an orchestration, the first thing that comes to mind is a large assembly of musicians, unified as they play through the pages of a single work of art. I'm often amazed at the sheer multitude of talent that is involved when I listen to a full orchestra working in harmony, without any sign of discrepancy. As you and I consider this collective magnificence, we begin to see that BizTalk orchestrations were aptly named. The server components in the orchestration engine compose a song of their own as they work through the lines of enterprise messages.

Okay, so maybe that's a bit dramatic, but the impressiveness of BizTalk orchestrations should still be held in high esteem. Microsoft, through the years, has continued to evolve the product into a fine system of data processing.

In this chapter, we'll take a closer, and rather basic, look at the orchestration process. You'll get an introduction to the Orchestration Designer and the various tools that you can use within it. And, of course, you'll put this knowledge to work with a sample application.

What Is an Orchestration?

The most basic definition of a BizTalk orchestration is that it is a collection of code that can be used to process data. Of course, there is more to the story than this. Realistically, orchestrations are a *huge* topic. One could almost write an entire book on the topic (and maybe someday I will). The central idea that you need to take away from this chapter is that orchestrations allows you to pull data from the messaging system and act upon it in a way that serves your enterprise. For instance, within the orchestration, you can perform database updates based on your message context, interact with other business processes (or orchestrations, for that matter), and modify the message itself with code.

From an architectural standpoint, the orchestration process is tied in to the BizTalk message box. Recall from Chapter 9 that the message box stands as a process between the receive port and the send port. To include the orchestration process, we must widen the scope of that flow to include this additional functionality. Figure 10-1 illustrates an overview of the messaging process including orchestrations.

The engine is distinctly tied to the message box and will "listen" for activity based on the subscriptions set up in the orchestration. You build the orchestration in the Orchestration Designer.

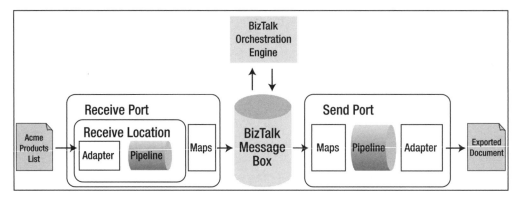

Figure 10-1. *Orchestrations within the messaging process*

Introducing the Orchestration Designer

To meet the Orchestration Designer, you need to pull it up within Visual Studio 2005. As a means to an end, you'll also set up the solution structure that you'll use in this chapter's example. You'll add the AcmeSchemas project, so that you'll have a ready-made schema at your disposal. You'll reuse the acmeProducts.csv file and the associated schema project that you created in Chapter 9.

Follow these steps to get started:

1. Start Visual Studio 2005

2. Create a new project by clicking File ➤ New ➤ Project.

3. Select Empty BizTalk Project and name it acmeOrchestrations.

4. Click File ➤ Add ➤ Existing Project.

5. Locate the AcmeSchemas.btproj file within the confines of the chapter9 folder and click OK.

6. Right-click the acmeOrchestrations project and select Add Reference.

7. Select the Projects tab and add the AcmeSchemas reference.

8. Click OK to exit. Your solution should look like Figure 10-2. You have a nearly complete solution for your investigatory purposes. The only thing missing is the orchestration.

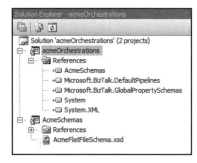

Figure 10-2. *Importing the AcmeSchemas project*

9. Right-click the `acmeOrchestrations` project, select Add ➤ New Item, and select Orchestration.

10. Save the new item as `acmeOrchestration.odx`.

After the orchestration loads, you'll find that the Visual Studio IDE has changed significantly. You have a few new panes to examine, as shown in Figure 10-3:

- The designer area with port surfaces

- An enhanced Toolbox window, complete with unique orchestration shapes

- The Orchestration View window

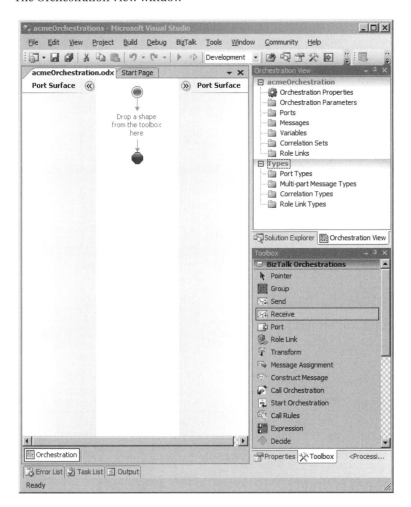

Figure 10-3. *The orchestration IDE*

Notice that the designer area has been divided into three sections: two port surfaces and an orchestration flowchart area, or "whiteboard." Generally, most developers will maintain their receive ports/requests on the left side and the send ports/responses on the right side of the whiteboard. This will, in theory, help you maintain some visible organization of your orchestrations. It's not a mandate, certainly, and you're free to put the ports on either side.

The power of the tool lies in the area between the port surfaces: the whiteboard. You'll drag-and-drop the various toolbox shapes that will enable you to route and manipulate the incoming messages. Figure 10-4 shows a comprehensive collection of the available toolbox shapes that you have at your disposal. Each of the components is a powerful tool, worthy of its own chapter. However, for the sake of brevity, Table 10-1 offers a summary of the tools.

Figure 10-4. *The BizTalk Orchestrations toolbox*

Table 10-1. *BizTalk Orchestration Tools*

Tool	Description
Group	Allows you to collect various shapes together into a collapsible region, in much the same way that code regions in Visual Studio allow you to collapse code. If your orchestration becomes large and unwieldy, consider organizing items with groups.
Send	Provides a mechanism for sending out a message.
Receive	Provides a mechanism for receiving a message.
Port	Provides the liaison between the BizTalk messages and the orchestration.
Role Link	Provides an abstract method of dynamically selecting which of your trading partners you would like to send or receive a message.
Transform	Allows you to map a message.

Tool	Description
Message Assignment	Nested within a Construct Message shape, allows you to create a message and assign values to it.
Construct Message	Creates a new instance of a message.
Call Orchestration	Synchronously calls another BizTalk orchestration.
Start Orchestration	Asynchronously calls another BizTalk orchestration.
Call Rules	Makes a call to a business policy.
Expression	Allows you to create an "in-line" C#-like language (XLang) coding block that can execute against the message.
Decide	Allows you to implement conditional logic in your orchestration flow.
Delay	Instructs the orchestration to pause for a set amount of time.
Listen	Provides a conditional branching mechanism that "listens" for the end of a Delay shape or the input of a message and turns flow control over to the branch that arrives first.
Parallel Actions	Gives you the opportunity to execute shapes in parallel to each other.
Loop	Provides a `while` loop within the orchestration flow.
Scope	Similar to coding scope, restricts transactions and error handling to a specified region.
Throw Exception	Throws an exception for bubbled-up error handling.
Compensate	Allows you to "undo" the effects of a transaction that has run its course by returning or resetting any resources that have been modified.
Suspend	Freezes an orchestration and bubbles up an error. While captured by a Suspend shape, the message will become resumable, as needed.
Terminate	Stops the orchestration and bubbles up an error. The message will be subsequently suspended; however, unlike with the Suspend shape, this message will be not be resumable.

As I've stated previously, these are very generic descriptions of the orchestration shapes. The best method for fully understanding the Orchestration Designer tools is to use them. You'll get started with that next, as you use a select few of the orchestration shapes in an example.

Building the Application

Before we dive into coding the sample application, let's first define what it is that we hope to accomplish with this particular task.

In the previous chapter, you implemented a messaging system for an imaginary retail organization. In that application, you had a product vendor, Acme Inc., who would supply you with a list of daily products and their availability. That list would arrive in comma-separated format. For this example, you will consume the product file, and based on the quantity of the product, forward the file to either a `replenishment` folder or a `discontinued` folder. You will need to load (or create) and subsequently save the following file in `c:\acme\chapter10` as `acmeProducts.csv`:

```
10001, Acme warp drive components, 123.56, 2
10013, Acme cloaking device, 234.99, 1
10021, Acme Time Travel Device, 855.99, 9
10045, Acme Personal Clone, 900.99, 0
```

As a reminder, if you're going to reuse the sample .csv file from the previous chapter, be sure to change the quantity to zero for the last product, as shown here.

Now let's jump back into Visual Studio 2005 and continue with the application you began building in the previous section. So far, you have an orchestration and schema project. However, you need to make a few changes to the flat file schema to accommodate some further functionality that you'll need when evaluating the incoming messages. You'll do that, and then add the XML disassembling pipeline from Chapter 9. Follow these steps:

1. Open the acmeFlatFileSchema file.

2. You need to change the type on the ProductQuantity element, so that you can promote it and use it as a computable integer. Highlight the ProductQuantity node and bring up the Properties window. Modify the Data Type to xs:int.

3. In order for the BizTalk messaging system to identify and work with the ProductQuantity field, you must declare that the field is a distinguished field. Right-click the ProductQuantity node and select Promote ➤ Show Promotions. On the Distinguished Fields tab, highlight the ProductQuantity element in the left panel and click the Add button, as shown in Figure 10-5.

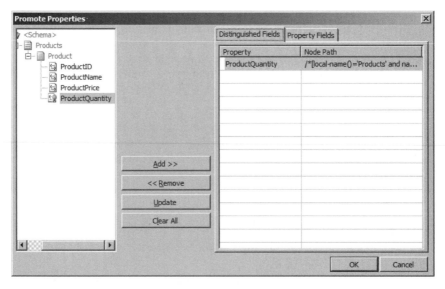

Figure 10-5. *Adding ProductQuantity as a distinguished field*

4. Save and build the acmeSchemas project.

5. Click File ➤ Add ➤ Existing Project.

6. Find and add the AcmePipelines.btproj file from the chapter9 folder.

7. Right-click the `acmeFlatFileSendPipeline` and delete the file. You won't be using it within the current project.

8. Open the `acmeFlatFileReceivePipeline` file.

9. Highlight the Flat File Disassembler and change the Document Schema property to refer to the new `acmeFlatFileSchema` reference.

10. Save and build the project.

Now that you have a basic structure in place for the message portion of the application, let's continue working with the `acmeOrchestration` file that you added earlier in the chapter.

Building the Orchestration

Before you begin dragging shapes out into the orchestration flow, we need to establish the basic premise of the project.

You will be accepting a series of XML product files into the messaging system, which have been disassembled by the custom pipeline. You would like to examine the `ProductQuantity` field, and if the quantity is greater than zero, you'll forward that to a file system folder called `replenishment`. If the quantity is zero, you'll forward the XML file to a folder named `discontinued`. So you know that you'll need to first create those directories.

1. In Windows Explorer, create three folders under `c:\chapter10`:

   ```
   C:\acme\chapter10\replenishment
   C:\acme\chapter10\discontinued
   C:\acme\chapter10\incoming
   ```

2. Ensure that the BizTalk service account has full control rights to the `chapter10` folder.

3. Open the `acmeOrchestration` file so that you're viewing the designer.

4. Switch to the Orchestration View tab.

Adding a Message

The orchestration is going to need a few items before you use any of the toolbox shapes. First and foremost, you need a message for the flow. You'll add a new message and its corresponding type to the orchestration.

1. Expand the Types node.

2. Right-click the Messages node and select New Message.

3. Change the identifier to `acmeFlatFileMessage`.

4. Click the Message Type drop-down list and expand the Schemas node. Click Select from Referenced Assembly.

5. When the artifact browser pops up, add the `AcmeFlatFileSchema`, and then click OK.

Adding Port Types

You now need to add a few port types, which will be the liaison, of sorts, to your message flow and the physical port that you'll create later.

1. Right-click the Port Types node and select New One-way Port Type.

2. Highlight PortType_1 and change its identifier in the Properties window to acmeReceivePortType.

3. You'll see that the Port Types node is expandable. Drill down into this node until Request (with the red exclamation point) is visible.

4. Click the Message Type drop-down list and drill down into the Schemas node.

5. Select the AcmeFlatFileSchema within the artifact browser, as when you added the message.

6. Add two more port types with the same properties and message type as acmeReceivePortType. Name your port types acmeDiscontinuedPortType and acmeReplenishmentPortType. Your types should look like those shown in Figure 10-6.

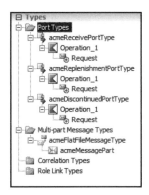

Figure 10-6. *Orchestration types in place*

Adding a Receive Shape

You've now come to the point where you can start using some orchestration shapes. First, you'll use a Receive shape.

1. Drag a Receive shape out to the whiteboard and place it between the start and stop points. You'll notice that a red exclamation point is visible on the shape. This lets you know that some configuration still needs to be done.

2. Change the name of the receive shape to Receive Message.

3. Set the Message property to acmeFlatFileMessage.

4. Set the Activate property to True.

5. Notice that the Operation property is still in need of configuration. If you click the drop-down list, you'll notice an absence of options. You need to bind this message-reception shape to an actual port now, if you want the shape to be fully configured. Right-click the leftmost port surface of the designer area and select New Port.

6. This port is in need of configuration, as expected. Open the Properties window for the new port.

7. Change the Identifier property of the port to acmeFlatFileReceivePort.

8. Click the drop-down list for the Port Type property. Find and select acmeReceivePortType.

9. Click and hold down the mouse on the port's green notch and drag it out to the notch of the Receive shape, as shown in Figure 10-7.

Figure 10-7. *Connecting the port to the Receive shape*

The red exclamation point should disappear, as the Receive shape is now fully configured.

Adding a Decide Shape

Now that you have the message safely arriving into the orchestration process, you need to perform an action based on its process.

1. Drag a Decide shape out to the whiteboard, just below the Receive shape. Your orchestration should look like Figure 10-8.

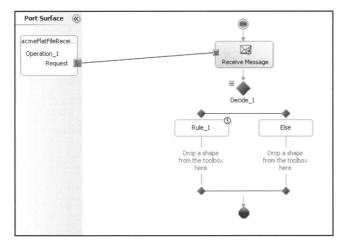

Figure 10-8. *Adding the Decide shape to the orchestration*

2. Highlight the `Rule_1` shape and bring up the Properties window.

3. Change the `Rule_1` name to `Replenishment`.

4. Click the ellipsis next to the Expression property.

5. Add the following code to the Expression window:

```
acmeFlatFileMessage.Product.ProductQuantity > 0
```

Adding a Send Shape for Replenishment

You need to forward any messages that have a quantity greater than zero to a distinct outbound send port. You'll create that functionality next.

1. Drag a Send shape to the empty region, just below the `Replenishment` rule.

2. Switch to the Properties window for the Send shape.

3. Change the name of the shape to `ReplenishmentSend`.

4. Click the Message drop-down list and select `acmeFlatFileMessage`.

5. Notice that the Send shape is in need of a port connection, in much the same way as required by your Receive shape earlier. Right-click the leftmost port surface and select New Port.

6. In the Properties window for the new send port, change the Communications Direction to Send.

7. Change the Identifier property from `Port_1` to `ReplenishmentSendPort`.

8. Click the Port Type drop-down list and, once again, drill down into the Port Types node and select the `acmeReplenishmentPortType`. Your Properties window for the send port should now look like Figure 10-9.

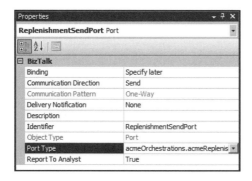

Figure 10-9. *Replenishment port properties*

9. Connect the Send shape to the newly created port, as you did with the Receive shape earlier.

Adding a Send Shape for Discontinued

You now need to turn your attention to the other branch of the Decide shape, wherein you must handle the possibility that the quantity is zero. When that situation occurs, you need to forward the message to another location: your discontinued folder.

1. Drag another Send shape out to the designer surface, just below the Else shape.

2. Open the Properties window of the shape and change its name to DiscontinuedSend.

3. Click the Message drop-down list and select acmeFlatFileMessage.

4. As you would expect, you need to create another port to facilitate the transfer of the message from the Discontinued branch to a physical folder location. Right-click the rightmost port surface and select New Port.

5. Highlight the new port and change its Identifier property to DiscontinuedSendPort.

6. Change the Communication Direction from Receive to Send.

7. Click the Port Type drop-down list, drill down into the Port Types node, and select acmeDiscontinuedPortType.

8. Connect the DiscontinuedSend shape to DiscontinuedSendPort by dragging the green notch to the appropriate connector.

Your orchestration is complete and should now look like Figure 10-10.

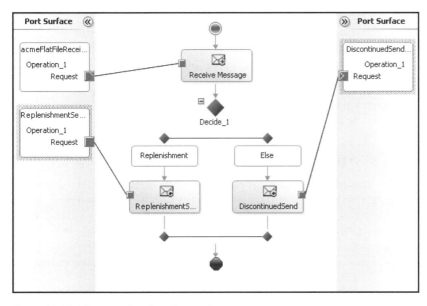

Figure 10-10. *The completed orchestration*

Deploying the Application

You've completed the assembly phase of the orchestration; however, you must configure a few items prior to deploying the application. You need to generate a strong name key, add it to all of the appropriate projects, and declare the application name for deployment.

1. Open the Visual Studio 2005 Command Prompt.

2. Change the directory to your `c:\acme\chapter10` folder.

3. Generate the key with the following command:

   ```
   sn -k keyfile.snk
   ```

   Now that you have a key waiting, you'll need to add it to each of the projects.

4. Right-click the orchestration project name and select Properties.

5. Select the Assembly option in the left panel.

6. Scroll down to Assembly Key File, and locate and add the key that you've just generated.

7. Expand the Configuration Properties node in the left panel.

8. Select the Deployment listing and change the application name to `chapter10`.

9. Click OK to accept the new configuration changes.

10. Select the properties for each of the other two projects, adding the key file and application name as you've done with the orchestration project.

11. You've completed the build and configuration of your application and now need to deploy it to the BizTalk Server. Deploy each of the projects to the server in the following order: `acmeSchemas`, `acmePipelines`, then `acmeOrchestrations`.

We're actually finished with the Visual Studio 2005 environment, and you can close it if you like.

Configuring and Starting the Application

You need to configure the application, connecting the virtual ports that you've created in your orchestration to real-world physical ports. You created a receive port and two send ports within `acmeOrchestration`. However, those were unbound ports that had no physical connection. In the next few steps, you'll create the file system ports and bind them to the orchestration ports as needed.

1. Start the BizTalk Server Administration Console application.

2. Expand the nodes in the left panel until your application, `chapter10`, is visible. You'll notice, by searching through the various folders, that your schema, pipeline, and orchestration have been properly deployed. You'll also notice that your orchestration is in a stopped state, as shown in Figure 10-11.

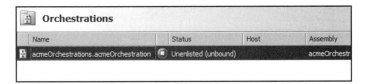

Figure 10-11. *The dormant orchestration*

Not only is the orchestration stopped, but it is missing the host assignment. You'll correct that and more in just a moment. First, you need to create the necessary ports.

Creating the Receive Port

Follow these steps to create the receive port for the application:

1. Right-click Receive Ports and select New ➤ One-Way Receive Port.

2. Change the name of the receive port to acmeFlatFileReceivePort.

3. Click Receive Locations in the left panel.

4. Click the New button to add a new location, as you have done in previous chapters.

5. Accept the default name, ReceiveLocation1.

6. Change the Type setting to File, and then click the Configure button.

7. In the File Transport Properties dialog box, click the Browse button and find the incoming folder that you created earlier in the chapter.

8. Change the File Mask setting to *.csv. The File Transport Properties dialog box should look like Figure 10-12.

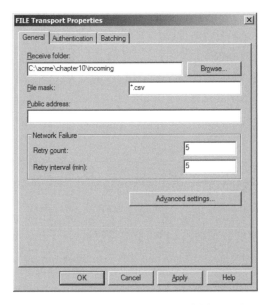

Figure 10-12. *Adding the incoming folder to the receive port*

9. Click OK to accept your settings and exit the dialog box.

10. Back in the Receive Location Properties dialog box, change the pipeline to the custom pipeline that you created earlier. The Receive Location Properties dialog box should look like Figure 10-13.

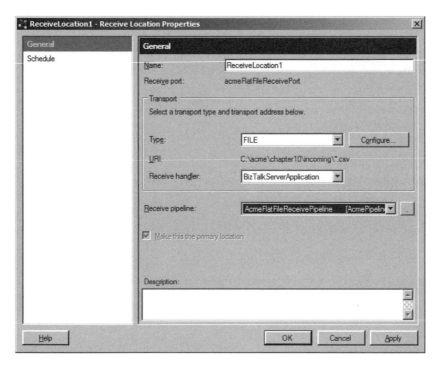

Figure 10-13. *Receive Location properties*

11. Click OK to accept the settings and return to the Port Properties dialog box.

12. Click OK to complete the port configuration.

13. In the application tree, notice that your newly formed receive location is in a Disabled state. You should fix that before proceeding. Right-click ReceiveLocation1 and select Enable.

Creating the Send Ports

You now need to create two physical send ports before you can bind your orchestration.

1. Right-click the Send Ports folder and select New ➤ Static One-Way Send Port.

2. Change the name of the new send port to acmeReplenishmentSendPort.

3. Change the Transport Type setting to File, and then click the Configure button (you could almost do this in your sleep by now).

4. In the File Transport Properties dialog box, click the Browse button and find the `replenishment` folder that you created earlier.

5. You won't be assembling the outgoing file to a `.csv` file as you did in Chapter 9, so leave the file name as set by default. Your transport settings should be as shown in Figure 10-14.

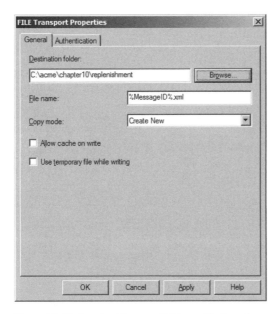

Figure 10-14. *Replenishment folder added to the send port*

6. Click OK to return to the Send Port Properties dialog box. You'll leave the send pipeline as PassThruTransmit, since you're not going to reassemble the individual product files at this time. Also note that you won't create any send port filters for this example. Because you're relying on the orchestration to subscribe and publish the messages, the filters are not necessary for this to work.

7. Click OK in the Send Port Properties dialog box to accept your configuration and return to the Administration Console.

8. Find your new send port and start the port by right-clicking and selecting Start. Your port should be started and ready, as shown in Figure 10-15.

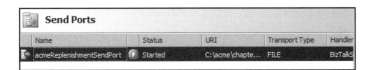

Figure 10-15. *Starting the replenishment send port*

9. You still have one more port to configure: the discontinued send port. Right-click the Send Ports folder and select New ➤ Static One-Way Send Port.

10. Change the name of the new send port to `acmeDiscontinuedSendPort`.

11. Change the Transport Type setting to File, and then click the Configure button (it's almost robotic at this point).

12. In the File Transport Properties dialog box, click the Browse button and find the `discontinued` folder that you created earlier.

13. Click OK to accept the transport settings.

14. You won't need a custom pipeline, so you'll leave the default PassThruTransmit in place. As before, you won't assign any filters to this port. Your send port properties should be as shown in Figure 10-16.

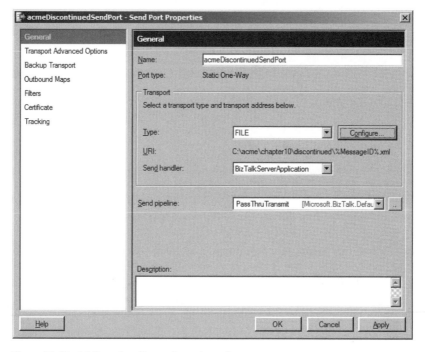

Figure 10-16. *Adding the discontinued send port*

15. Back in the console application, you'll notice that this port also needs to be started. Right-click the new port and select Start.

Binding the Ports

You've created all of the necessary ports for the input and output of your physical message files. Now you need to bind them to the orchestration.

1. Click the Orchestrations folder so that you can view your stopped orchestration.

2. Right-click the orchestration and select Properties.

3. Click the Bindings option in the left panel.

4. Change the Host setting to `BizTalkServerApplication`.

5. Under Receive Ports, change the <none> to the receive port that you created earlier, `acmeFlatFileReceivePort`.

6. For the `ReplenishmentSendPort`, change the send port from <none> to `acmeReplenishmentSendPort`.

7. Similarly, change the send port for the `DiscontinuedSendPort` from <none> to `acmeDiscontinuedSendPort`. Your orchestration bindings should look like Figure 10-17.

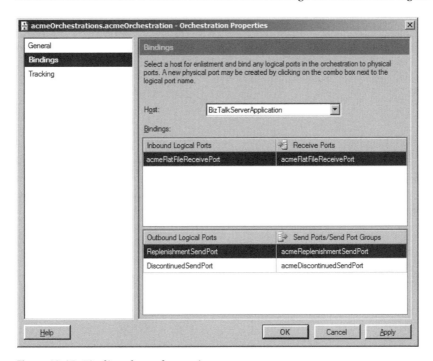

Figure 10-17. *Binding the orchestration ports*

8. Right-click the orchestration and select Start. The orchestration will now bind to the appropriate ports and set its status to Started.

9. And now for the moment of truth! Find the `acmeProducts.csv` file that you've used and drop it into the incoming folder.

After a moment or two, the orchestration will process your messages and should dump three files into the `replenishment` folder and a single file into the `discontinued` folder. If you open the lone file in the `discontinued` folder, you will see that, yes, indeed, the `ProductQuantity` is equal to zero, as shown in Figure 10-18.

You've successfully fulfilled all of the application's initial requirements, having routed the product files according to their distinguished field, `ProductQuantity`.

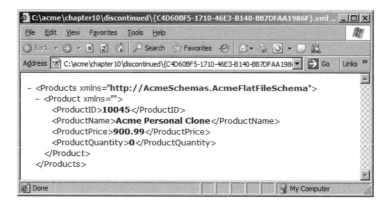

Figure 10-18. *The properly routed discontinued product file*

Summary

Obviously, there is much more to the world of orchestrations. In this very limited example, you've been exposed to a few shapes, expressions, and the creation of "virtual" ports within the Orchestration Designer. In the next chapter, you'll build upon this foundational lesson as we delve deeper into a few of the more advanced orchestration topics.

■ ■ ■

CHAPTER 11

Advanced Orchestrations

In the previous chapter, you were introduced to BizTalk orchestrations. As I noted in that chapter, what you've learned so far is only a scratch on the surface of the product's true capabilities. This chapter covers two other areas of orchestration functionality, which you may eventually require in your professional endeavors. First, we will investigate the subject of correlation and message routing. Then we'll move on to a demonstration centered around the handling of failed messages.

Correlation

In the previous examples, you processed an incoming message by simply routing it to an outgoing port. You weren't really concerned with what happened to the message after it had left the send port, as your business use for the message had been met. But what if you needed to send a message out and then receive it back for further processing? Let's discuss a situation that would reflect that particular scenario.

Suppose that, back at Acme Inc., you've been asked to construct a routing application that will facilitate an external authorization process for purchases over $1,000. You'll have an inbound message that you accept on an input port. Based on the dollar value of the price element, you'll either send the message straight to a final send port or you'll direct it to an external authorization process. If the message is sent for approval, you want the orchestration to "pause" and wait for the same message to return before it continues processing, as illustrated in Figure 11-1. To accomplish that, you'll need to create what is known as a *correlation set*.

Essentially, a correlation set allows you to declare that a promoted property will be used for identification on any related messages that leave and return to the orchestration. Portions of the orchestration must subscribe to this correlation set so that the BizTalk engine is able to differentiate between an original message and one that is a continuation of work previously done.

Undoubtedly, some of you are looking at the diagram in Figure 11-1 and thinking, "What if the message never comes back to the orchestration?" Or possibly you're wondering, "What happens to the orchestration while it's waiting for the message? Does it stay in state or does it save itself somehow?" And both are excellent queries and certainly applicable to your message life cycle. The Listen shape allows you to set a timeout on the activity at hand. So if the accounting department doesn't approve the order on time, the orchestration will time out and move on. But those message orchestrations that are patiently waiting for their delivered messages to return home enter what is known as *dehydration*.

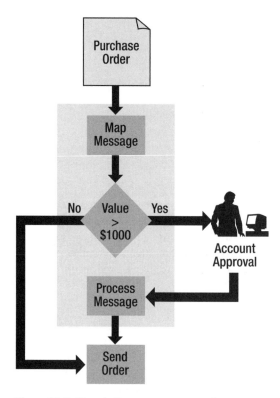

Figure 11-1. *Correlation pattern example*

■**Note** If, for some reason, a message returns and the orchestration has terminated, you'll end up with what has been affectionately termed a *zombie*. For information about ways to deal with that devious situation, see the MSDN article at `http://msdn2.microsoft.com/en-us/library/aa561361.aspx`.

Understanding Dehydration and Persistence Points

Dehydration is one of the most misunderstood orchestration topics and, ultimately, it's not that hard to comprehend.

Imagine that your BizTalk Server is processing 1,000 messages a minute. Not only is it receiving and mapping, it is also sending those messages to an external application process that will approve or deny them based on business criteria. However, that process could possibly be a time-consuming one. Should you ask BizTalk to simply wait, with all of those orchestration instances idling and chewing up your valuable resources? Certainly not!

Instead of just waiting, the orchestration will dehydrate, and the state of the instance is taken out of memory and stored in SQL Server. BizTalk does this to free up valuable resources for other processes. A special subscription will be created for the dehydrated instance of the orchestration. This subscription will monitor the BizTalk message box for context properties that match your unique correlation ID. When the subscription comes across that message, the orchestration will "wake up," and the state of the instance will be taken out of the database and reconstituted in memory. The point at which the orchestration will, essentially, come alive is known as a *persistence point*.

Persistence points are created throughout the orchestration and provide a method of bookmarking activities, so that when the orchestration is revisited (for correlation, for example), BizTalk will pick up right at the last persistence point. A send port is automatically a persistence point, and when you think of it in terms of correlation, that makes perfect sense. These restore points also provide an avenue of recovery for orchestrations in the event that the service or hosting computer suffers a catastrophic failure.

Building the Correlation Application

Now that you have a basic understanding of correlation concepts, let's move on to the actual implementation. The basic premise of the sample application is laid out in Figure 11-1. You'll build the application around the concept that a message will come in, go out for approval, return for processing, and finally exit the orchestration at its final destination.

Creating the Schemas Project

As usual, you'll start by creating an XML schema.

1. Start Visual Studio 2005.

2. Choose to create an Empty BizTalk Server Project. Name it `Acme.Schemas` and save it in `c:\acme\chapter11`. Create a solution directory named `chapter 11`.

3. Click File ➤ Add ➤ New Project.

4. Add another Empty BizTalk Server Project, naming this one `Acme.Orchestrations`.

5. Create the following XML file and save it as `order.xml` in the `chapter 11` folder.

```
<Order>
  <OrderID>101</OrderID>
  <ProductID>A0B111222</ProductID>
  <OrderQuantity>1</OrderQuantity>
  <ProductPrice>499.99</ProductPrice>
  <Status>New</Status>
</Order>
```

6. Right-click the `Acme.Schemas` project name in the Solution Explorer and select Add ➤ Add Generated Items.

7. Create an XML schema, using the sample XML file as the input instance file. (Refer to Chapter 6 if you need help generating the file.)

8. Modify the `OrderID` and `OrderQuantity` data types so that they are `xs:int` types. Your current schema should look like Figure 11-2.

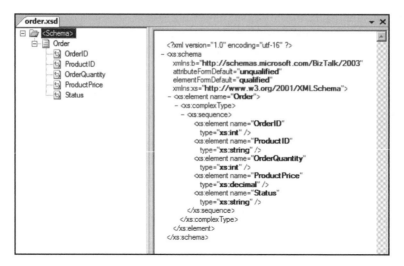

Figure 11-2. *The sample order schema*

9. The orchestration will need to have a property by which it can "track" the message, so you need to promote a property. Right-click the OrderID node and select Promote ➤ Quick Promotion. You'll be asked to confirm that you want to add the property schema. Select OK to continue.

10. Distinguish, rather than promote, the ProductPrice and Status nodes. You'll be using those elements later for routing. (See Chapter 10 for help on distinguishing fields.)

■**Note** The primary difference between promoted properties and distinguished fields is that promoted properties can be used for routing, correlation, and tracking messages based on the indicated (or promoted) property. A distinguished field value can still be accessed from within an orchestration, and if your integration application requires only that functionality, you'll want to choose distinguished fields over promoted properties, as they are less taxing to system resources.

---

11. Build (but don't deploy) the Acme.Schemas project.

If you don't build the Schemas project before proceeding, you will not have access to the Acme schemas.

Building the Orchestration

You will be using only a single schema in this sample application, so you can move on to the orchestration now.

1. Right-click the `Acme.Orchestrations` project name in the Solution Explorer and select Add ➤ New Item.

2. Select Orchestration Files in the left pane and BizTalk Orchestrations in the right pane. Save your orchestration as `OrderProcessing.odx`.

3. Right-click the `Acme.Orchestrations` project name and select Add Reference.

4. Select the Projects tab and add the `order` schema from the `Acme.Schemas` project.

5. Switch over to the Orchestration View window. Right-click the Messages folder and select New Message, as shown in Figure 11-3.

Figure 11-3. *Adding a new message to the orchestration*

6. Change the Identifier property of the new message to `order`.

7. Click the drop-down list for the Message Type property of the new message. Expand the Schemas node and click Select from Referenced Assembly. Find and use the `Acme.Schemas order` schema, as shown in Figure 11-4.

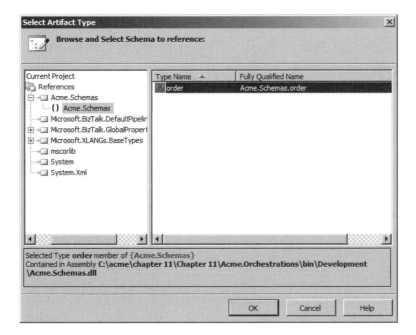

Figure 11-4. *Adding the order message type*

Configuring the Receive Port

Now you're ready to add some shapes to your orchestration. You'll begin with the Receive shape.

1. Drag a Receive shape out onto the orchestration designer.

2. Switch to the Properties window of the shape and change its name to ReceiveOrder.

3. Click the drop-down list for the Message property and select order.

4. Set the Activate property to True.

5. Right-click the left port surface of the designer area and select New Configured Port.

6. Add an XML receive port (as you did in Chapter 10). Name the port OrderIn and the port type OrderInType. This will be a one-way, receive port. You will specify the appropriate port binding information later.

7. Connect the Receive Port shape to the Receive shape, as shown in Figure 11-5.

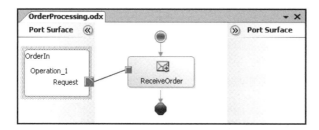

Figure 11-5. *The Receive shape is fully configured.*

Implementing the Decision Point

If you recall from the application design discussion earlier, you need to implement a decision point within the orchestration to route the messages based on the ProductPrice element.

1. Drag a Decide shape to the whiteboard, just below the Receive shape.

2. Rename the Rule_1 block to LargeOrder.

3. Double-click LargeOrder to bring up the Expression window. Add the following expression to the code box, and then click OK to continue:

```
order.ProductPrice > 1000
```

Orders coming in that have a price greater than $1,000 will follow the path to the left, while those satisfying the Else logic will roll down the path to the right, as shown in Figure 11-6.

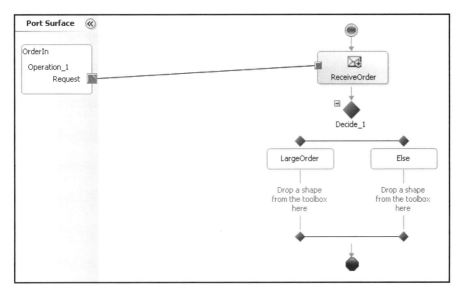

Figure 11-6. *Implementing the Decide shape*

Configuring the Send Port for "Small" Orders

Let's first add the send functionality for those orders whose pricing is below $1,000 and so will not need further approval. You're not really interested in taking any kind of business action against those particular orders; you just want to move them along the process. You'll do that by adding a send port to the Else branch of your Decision shape.

1. Drag a Send shape out to the whiteboard, just below the Else shape.

2. In the Properties window, change the Message property by selecting order from the drop-down list.

3. Right-click the rightmost port surface and add a new configured port. Name the outbound port MinorOrderOut. This port will be a one-way send port that will have its port bindings specified later. Make sure you select sending for the port direction.

4. Connect the MinorOrderOut port to the Send shape, as shown in Figure 11-7.

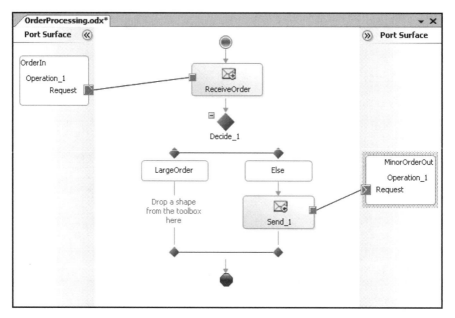

Figure 11-7. *Lesser-priced orders port configured and attached*

5. Change the Name property of Send_1 to SendMinorOut.

You now have a destination for your smaller orders that will not need to be involved in the approval process.

Adding Correlation Information

Before configuring the send and receive functionality for orders whose pricing is above $1,000, you need to add the correlation information so that the messages will have the appropriate context when passing out of (and back into) the orchestration. You'll do that by adding a correlation type and then the corresponding correlation set.

1. In the Orchestration View window, right-click the Correlation Types folder and select New Correlation Type.

2. Expand the Acme.Schemas.PropertySchema node. Highlight the OrderId node and select Add to move it to the right pane, as shown in Figure 11-8. Click OK to finish.

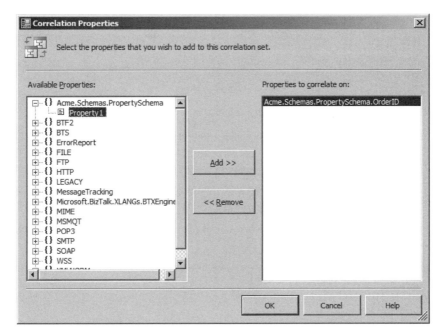

Figure 11-8. *Adding the correlation type*

3. Right-click the Correlation Sets folder in the Orchestration View window and select New Correlation Set.

4. In the Properties window for the new set, click the Correlation Type drop-down list and add the correlation type that you just created.

Configuring the Correlation Process

You now have a working and waiting correlation set and type. To use those, you'll need to create the appropriate Send and Receive shapes that will take advantage of the newfound ability. If an incoming order satisfies the "greater than $1,000" requirement, you'll need to export the file to a send port and create a corresponding receive port to receive it after the accounting department has updated the file.

You'll then need to handle the logic for approved and denied orders. When the order is sent out for approval, the corresponding <Status> element will be modified to either Approved or Denied. Based on that status code, you'll need to take the appropriate actions. In the current scenario, you'll simply dump approved orders into one folder and denied orders into another.

1. Add a Send shape, just below the LargeOrder shape.

2. Set the Message property of the shape to order.

3. Change the Name property to SendLargeOut.

4. Click the Initializing Correlation Sets drop-down list and select the only option listed.

5. Right-click the leftmost port surface and create another configured send port as you did earlier. Save this port as OrderApprovalSend and elect to specify the bindings later.

6. Connect the newly created Send shape to your new port.

7. Drag a Receive shape out to the whiteboard, just below SendLargeOut.

8. Change the Name property to ReceiveLargeIn.

9. Click the Following Correlation Sets drop-down list and select the only option listed.

10. Set the Message property to order.

11. Right-click the leftmost port surface and create a new configured receive port. Name it OrderApprovalReceive and elect to specify the bindings later.

12. Connect OrderApprovalReceive to the ReceiveLargeIn shape. Your current orchestration should look like Figure 11-9.

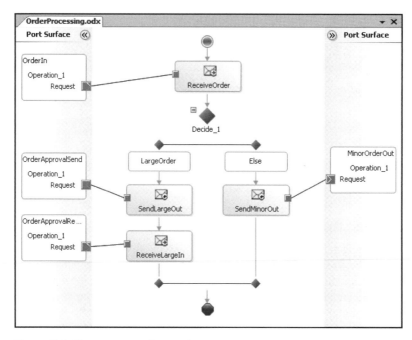

Figure 11-9. *The current orchestration*

13. Drag another Decide shape out and place it just below the ReceiveLargeIn shape (see Figure 11-10 for visual reference).

14. Change the Name property of Rule_1 to Approved.

15. Double-click the Approved shape and add the following code in the Expression window:

```
order.Status == "Approved"
```

16. Drag a Send shape out to the designer, just below the Approved shape.

17. Change the Name property of the Send shape to `SendToApproved`.

18. Select `order` from the Message property drop-down list for the Send shape.

19. As you would expect, you need to create another send port on the leftmost port surface. Add a configured send port and save it as `OrderApproved`. You'll specify the bindings later.

20. Connect the port to the Send shape.

21. Under the Else shape of your second Decide shape, place another Send shape.

22. Change the name to `SendToDenied`.

23. Set the Message property to `order`, as you have done with previous Send shapes.

24. Create a send port on the rightmost port surface. Name it `OrderDenied` and choose to specify the bindings later. Your orchestration should look like Figure 11-10.

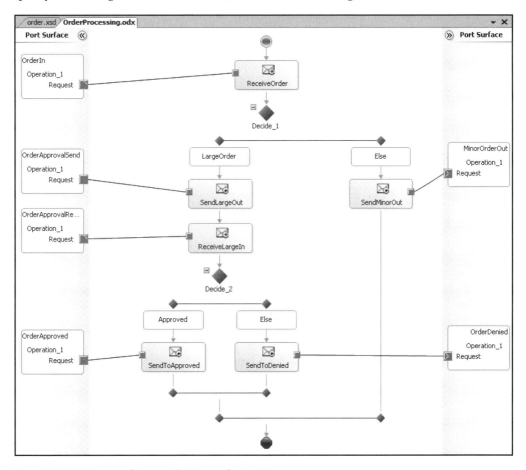

Figure 11-10. *The complete correlation orchestration*

25. Connect the Send shape to the new port.

That's it! Your correlation orchestration is complete.

Deploying the Correlation Application

Now you can take care of the usual housekeeping chores, and then deploy the application.

1. Create a strong name key for the solution and add it to both of the projects. (Refer to earlier chapters for help, if needed.)

2. Add Chapter11 as the application name in your deployment configuration for both of the solution projects.

3. Deploy the schema and orchestration to the BizTalk engine.

You're actually finished with your work in Visual Studio 2005 for this particular application. If you want to close the IDE, you're free to do so.

Binding the Ports

Before you jump into the BizTalk Administration Console, you need to take care of some application-specific tasks. If you were keeping count, you may have noticed that you created six ports that will send and receive your order message. You need to create those physical locations on the hard drive and give your directories the appropriate access permissions.

Under the c:\Acme\Chapter11 folder, create the following subfolders:

- OrderIn

- MinorOrderOut

- ApprovalWaiting

- ApprovalSubmitted

- OrderApproved

- OrderDenied

And now the fun part: binding all of these folders to your orchestration ports! It's not as bad as you might think, and it makes for great BizTalk practice. You'll create the ports and then bind them to the appropriate orchestration locations. There should be a logical assignment to the ports, and you'll find that it's quite easy to bind ports when you use corresponding naming schemes.

1. Start the BizTalk Administration Console and expand your Chapter11 application. You should see your schema and orchestration.

2. Right-click Receive Ports and create a new one-way receive port. Name the receive port ReceiveOrderMessage.

3. Create a new receive location with the following properties:

   - Name: ReceiveOrderLocation

   - Transport Type: File (C:\acme\chapter11\orderin)

   - Receive Pipeline: XMLReceive

4. Right-click Send Ports and create a new static, one-way send port with the following properties:

   - Name: `MinorOrderPort`

   - Transport Type: File (`C:\acme\chapter11\MinorOrderOut`)

   - Send Pipeline: PassThruTransmit

5. Create another static, one-way send port with the following properties:

   - Name: `ApprovalWaitingPort`

   - Transport Type: File (`C:\acme\chapter11\ApprovalWaiting`)

   - Send Pipeline: XMLTransmit

6. Create a new receive port and receive location with the following properties:

   - Port Name: `ApprovalSubmittedPort`

   - Location Name: `ApprovalSubmittedLocation`

   - Transport Type: File (`C:\acme\chapter11\ApprovalSubmitted`)

   - Receive Pipeline: XMLReceive

7. Create a static, one-way send port with the following properties:

   - Name: `OrderApprovedPort`

   - Transport Type: File (`C:\acme\chapter11\OrderApproved`)

   - Send Pipeline: PassThruTransmit

8. Create a final static, one-way send port with the expected properties:

   - Name: `OrderDeniedPort`

   - Transport Type: File (`C:\acme\chapter11\OrderDenied`)

   - Send Pipeline: PassThruTransmit

9. Locate the `OrderProcessing` orchestration.

10. Right-click the orchestration and select Properties.

11. Select Bindings in the left panel.

12. Assign the appropriate Host property. Leaving it blank would be bad.

13. Bind the ports, as shown in Figure 11-11:

    - `OrderIn` to `ReceiveOrderMessage`

    - `OrderApprovalReceive` to `ApprovalSubmittedPort`

    - `OrderApprovalSend` to `ApprovalWaitingPort`

- `MinorOrderOut` to `MinorOrderPort`

- `OrderApproved` to `OrderApprovedPort`

- `OrderDenied` to `OrderDeniedPort`

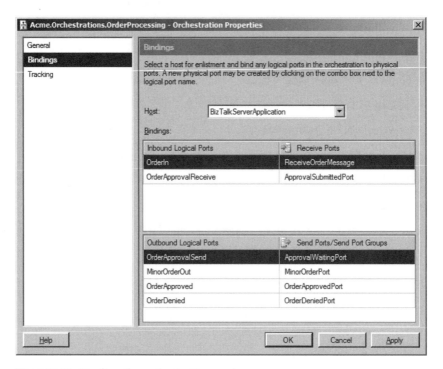

Figure 11-11. *Binding the orchestration ports*

14. Right-click the orchestration and select Enlist.

15. Right-click the `Chapter11` application folder and select Start. Clicking Start allows you to shortcut the starting/enabling of all those individual ports and simply get things up and running.

If you click through each of the folders, you should find that everything is running and ready.

Testing the Correlation Application

So now you're finally ready to test! Along the way, you'll take a look at the background dehydration process.

Simulating an Order

First, you need to simulate a purchase order for more than $1,000.

1. Find the order.xml file and verify that the price is less than $1,000.

2. Copy the file and place the copy into the OrderIn folder. After a moment, BizTalk will consume the message and process it.

3. Flip over to the MinorOrderOut folder, and you should find the XML file waiting there.

4. Change the price of the original order.xml to a value greater than $1,000.

5. Copy the file and drop it into the OrderIn folder.

After a moment, the file will be processed and pushed out to the ApprovalWaiting folder. You'll need to do some hands-on work with the XML before moving it along the process. But before you do that, I want to show you the background dehydration process.

Viewing the Dehydrated Orchestration

When BizTalk dehydrates the waiting orchestration, you'll find the status on the Group Overview page in the BizTalk Administration Console, as shown in Figure 11-12. To get to the overview page, click Start ➤ Programs ➤ Microsoft BizTalk Server 2006 ➤ BizTalk Server Administration ➤ BizTalk Group Node. Then press F5 to refresh the view.

Work in Progress	
Running service instances	1
- Dehydrated orchestrations	1
- Retrying and idle ports	0
- Ready service instances	0
- Scheduled service instances	0

Figure 11-12. *The dehydrated orchestration available for investigation*

For more information, you can drill down into the dehydrated instance and click the option to open the Orchestration Debugger. You'll notice as you click each of the individual Action Name rows that the corresponding orchestration shape is highlighted. If you step through each of the shapes, you'll be able to see where BizTalk did indeed send out the message on the correct port and subsequently went into a waiting state on the Receive shape, as shown in Figure 11-13.

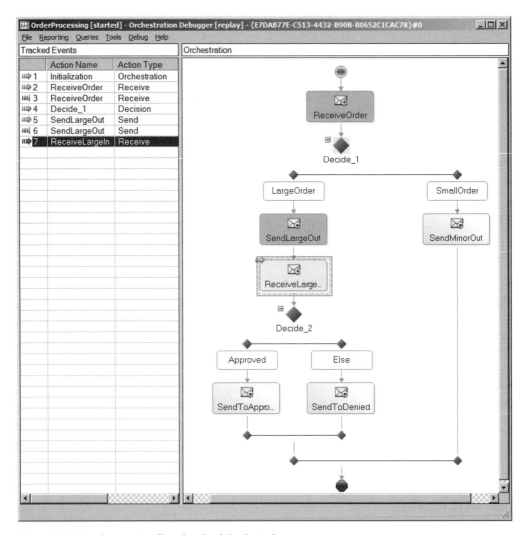

Figure 11-13. *Orchestration flow for the dehydrated message*

Simulating Approval

To see the final part of the application at work, you need an approved order.

1. Open the ApprovalWaiting folder and edit the XML file so that the status is Approved:

```
<?xml version="1.0" encoding="utf-8"?><Order>
  <OrderID>101</OrderID>
  <ProductID>A0B111222</ProductID>
  <OrderQuantity>1</OrderQuantity>
  <ProductPrice>1499.99</ProductPrice>
  <Status>Approved</Status>
</Order>
```

2. Drag-and-drop the file to the `ApprovalSubmitted` folder.

BizTalk will now rehydrate the orchestration and continue with the rest of the application as designed. If you select the `OrderApproved` folder, you should find the file waiting.

Also, if you return to the BizTalk Administration Console and refresh the Group Overview page, you'll find that the orchestration was indeed hydrated and processed, and no more outstanding work remains, as shown in Figure 11-14.

Work in Progress	
Running service instances	0
- Dehydrated orchestrations	0
- Retrying and idle ports	0
- Ready service instances	0
- Scheduled service instances	0

Figure 11-14. *The orchestration has hydrated and cleared.*

Dehydration is a powerful tool that BizTalk has built into the process. Knowing that you can resume an orchestration, either on purpose or in recovery, makes BizTalk a stronger integration product. Now when you receive a message from a trading partner, not only will you need to receive it only once, but if something catastrophic happens, you'll be able to retain the message and continue processing it right where you left off when the stuff hit the fan.

Failed Messages

If you've written software for longer than 15 minutes, then you've undoubtedly discovered that things don't always go your way. You could spend weeks in architectural design, coding standards, and meticulous coding cycles, and yet it could all coming crashing down because of one stupid missing semicolon. We've all been there.

It's quite possible that during the course of working through this book, a message or two has gone astray. Perhaps it became suspended and didn't quite achieve the desired results. I've been smitten by the demo gods enough to realize that a few readers will undoubtedly need to endure the process of finding the suspended messages and investigating what went wrong. It's a frustrating process, and you'll want to pull your hair out (assuming that you have some to start with). Fortunately, BizTalk helps us along in this investigation process.

New to BizTalk Server 2006 is the ability to generate an error report message when a message is suspended. It actually becomes something that you can filter and subscribe to via an orchestration. You can create an application that will handle failed messages and take an appropriate course of action. And that's exactly what you'll do for this final demonstration.

Creating an Application with Routable Errors

For a demonstration of how to filter for errors, you need to have some errors. This is an easy task. You'll simply create a receive port that accepts any XML file into the message box, but you won't create a corresponding subscription (send port or orchestration) for the message. So, in effect, you'll strand the message in the message box, and BizTalk will recognize that and throw an error. To flag that message as routable on error, you need to toggle a selection in the receive port, as you'll see in a moment.

1. Under the C:\acme\chapter11 folder that you created earlier, create a subfolder and name it BadReceivePort.

2. Create another folder under BadReceivePort and name it In. The folder should now be located at C:\acme\chapter11\BadReceivePort\In.

3. Create a second folder under BadReceivePort and name it ErrorsForwarded.

4. Start the BizTalk Administration Console and expand the Applications node.

5. Right-click Application and select New ➤ Application. Name your application BadPortReceive. Click OK to create the application.

6. In your new application, right-click Receive Ports and create a new one-way receive port. Name the port BadReceivePort.

7. In the Receive Port Properties dialog box, select the Enable Routing for Failed Messages check box, as shown in Figure 11-15.

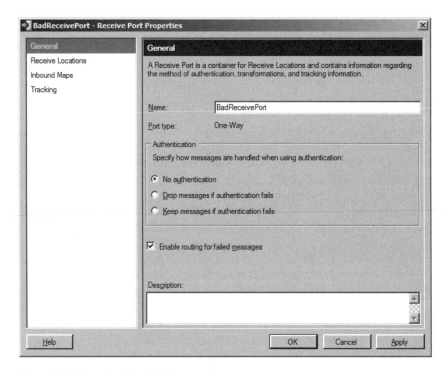

Figure 11-15. *Routing for failed messages*

8. Create a receive location for the port. Name it BadReceiveLocation. Set its Transport Type to File (C:\acme\chapter11\BadReceivePort\In) and its Receive Pipeline to XMLReceive, as shown in Figure 11-16. Then click OK.

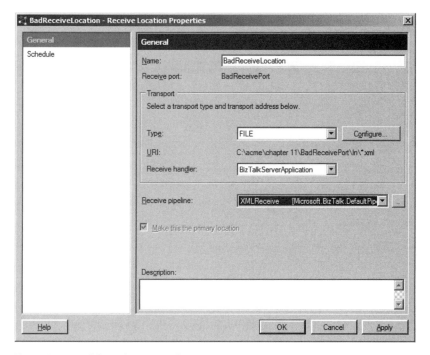

Figure 11-16. *Adding the receive location*

You're not going to do anything else with this port or its functionality, which is kind of the point of the matter—you want things to blow up.

Building the Handler Application

Before you turn the "bad" port on, let's create an application that will handle stranded messages.

1. Start a new instance of Visual Studio 2005.

2. Create an Empty BizTalk Server Project and name it `FailedMessageHandler`. Create the application in the `C:\acme\chapter11\BadReceivePort` folder.

3. After the project loads, right-click the project name and add a new orchestration, saving it as `FailedMessageOrchestration`.

Starting the Orchestration

You need to create a generic XML document message type within the orchestration. Since you know that you're going to receive an error message type in the shape of an XML document, that's really all you're concerned with at the moment.

1. Right-click Messages in the Orchestration View window and select New Message.

2. Change the message Identifier property to `FailedMessage`.

3. For the Message Type, find System.Xml.XmlDocument under the .NET Classes node, as shown in Figure 11-17.

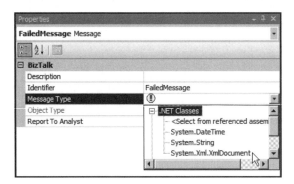

Figure 11-17. *Adding the XmlDocument type*

Configuring the Receive Port

Now that you have a useful message type, you need to get these failed messages into the orchestration. You also need to retrieve these failed messages from the BizTalk message box. You'll need to create a "direct" port, which you haven't done in earlier examples.

1. Drag a Receive shape onto the designer. Name it GetFailed.

2. Set the Activate property to True.

3. Set the Message property to FailedMessage.

4. Right-click the leftmost port surface and select New Configured Port.

5. As the wizard progresses, name the port RetrieveFailedPort and set the port type as RetrieveFailedPortType. When asked to specify the port direction, this is where you'll part ways from the ordinary ports that you have created previously. You are indeed "Always Receiving Messages" on this port, but you need to select Direct from the Port Binding drop-down list. Other options will appear, but you're only concerned with selecting the first. This will allow you to filter by an expression, rather than by a specified receive port. Click Next, and then click Finish.

6. You need to add the required expression to the Receive shape so that the filter will be applied within the orchestration. Highlight the Receive shape in the designer, locate the Filter Expression property, and click the ellipsis to bring up the editor. Select ErrorReport.ErrorType in the Property column and add FailedMessage to the Value column, as shown in Figure 11-18.

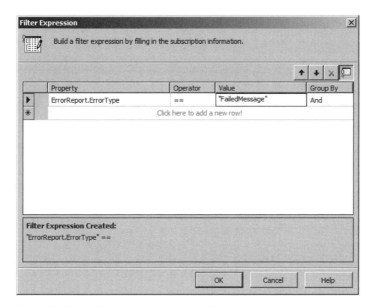

Figure 11-18. *Adding the appropriate filter expression*

7. Connect the Direct port on the left port surface to the Receive shape.

You have now added the necessary functionality to get the failed messages into the orchestration.

Configuring the Send Port

You could take a variety of actions based on the presence of an errant file: e-mail an administrator, store the file, FTP it to a reserved location, and so on. The possibilities are endless and depend on your business needs, but for the current and simple application, you're simply going to route the failed message out of the BizTalk message box and into a folder on the hard drive. A clutter-free message box is always a good thing.

1. Drag a Send shape out to the whiteboard, just below the Receive shape.

2. Change the Name property to `SendFailed`.

3. Set the Message property to `FailedMessage`.

4. Right-click the rightmost port surface and create a new configured port.

5. Name the port `SendErrorPort` and set the port type to `SendErrorPortType`.

6. Change the port direction to sending and retain the selection to specify port bindings later.

7. Click Next, and then click Finish to exit the wizard.

Deploying the Application

Take the familiar steps to deploy your handler application.

1. Create a strong name key for the application and assign it to the project properties.

2. Modify the application name to FailedMessageHandler within the deployment properties.

3. Build and deploy the project.

Binding the Ports

Now finish up by binding the ports.

1. Start the BizTalk Administration Console.

2. Locate and expand your new application.

3. Right-click Send Ports and select New ➤ Static One-Way Send Port.

4. Name the port SendFailedMessages. Create a File type transport that points to the ErrorsForwarded folder that you created earlier. Leave the Send Pipeline setting as PassThruTransmit, and click OK to create the port.

5. Enlist and start the new send port.

6. Open the Orchestrations folder and bring up the Properties dialog box for your new orchestration.

7. Select the Bindings option and assign the new send port to the orchestration's logical port, as shown in Figure 11-19. Don't forget to add your host application, as shown in the figure. (That omission has nailed me a few times and is very frustrating.) Click OK to exit the Orchestration Properties dialog box.

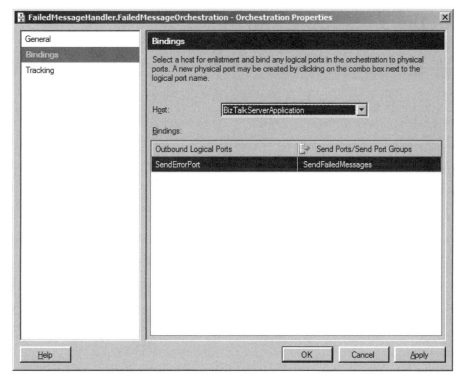

Figure 11-19. *Connecting your physical and logical ports*

8. Right-click the orchestration and select Enlist and then Start.

Testing the Handler Application

The orchestration is now monitoring your message box for errors. So let's be a good sport and provide one!

1. In the BadPortReceive application, enable the receive location, which will essentially kick off our process.

2. Drop an XML file (such as order.xml from the previous example) into the C:\acme\chapter11\BadReceivePort\In folder.

BizTalk will attempt to route this message, but will be unable to find a corresponding subscription for it. It should error out, and your new orchestration should take over and move it into the ErrorsForwarded folder. You have successfully routed a failed message!

I've included this final application because I feel very strongly that you should always provide some form of contingency plan for failed messages. They will happen to even the best of us. It's just a matter of when and where. Having a process in place to notify you in the event of a message failure will help to make your BizTalk implementations a stable and stress-free process.

Summary

In this chapter, we have only scratched the surface of orchestration possibilities. I encourage you to follow up on the topics glossed over here. Again, I suggest *Pro BizTalk Server 2006* (Apress, ISBN: 1-59059-699-4) as your next book after this one.

I also recommend that you continue to modify the sample applications within this chapter. As an entertaining and informative task, create the functionality necessary to e-mail failed messages from within the recent orchestration. And be sure to share the knowledge with others by blogging and publishing your experience with BizTalk orchestrations.

CHAPTER 12

■■■

Business Rules

So far, you've built quite a few sample projects that have accomplished a variety of business-related tasks. At the end of each demo, you saved, built, and deployed your work. But what if you wanted to make some changes to processing logic contained within an orchestration? You would need to modify, build, and redeploy the orchestration. And while it's not an incredibly difficult process, it can be a bit frustrating if you're redeploying because of a simple change, such as an interest rate in a loan-processing orchestration.

As developers and database administrators, we are responsible for making the back-end data processes available to the world via software. And the software methods by which we compute that data is ever-changing. What we need is a methodology for implementing dynamic logic processing against our BizTalk messages. This is where the business rules engine comes into the picture.

In this chapter, we'll take a closer, and rather basic, look at the business rules process. You'll get an introduction to the business rules engine, and then take a quick look at the Business Rule Composer. The rest of the chapter is devoted to building a sample application that includes a business rule.

What Is the Business Rules Engine?

The business rules engine (BRE) is a key component of the BizTalk package. It provides a venue in which enterprise-specific logic can be called into play when processing messages. For instance, Figure 12-1 illustrates how an ever-changing qualifier business process could be applied to an incoming message.

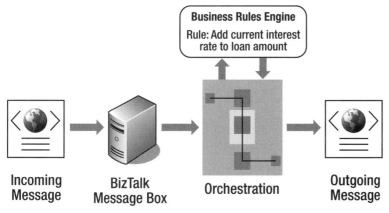

Figure 12-1. *Overview of a simple rules application*

In the example in Figure 12-1, the BRE is called from within an orchestration. However, that is not the only avenue of access for the BRE. You can also use an API implementation of the product, as illustrated in Figure 12-2.

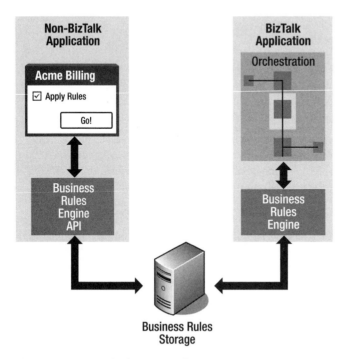

Figure 12-2. *Using the business rules engine*

The fact that the API can be called from anywhere really sheds a different light on the BRE. It can truly become an enterprise-specific resource, rather than something that is isolated to BizTalk orchestrations (you'll still need the BizTalk Server licensing, however). But what exactly is a business rule? Is it code? Is it a class method?

Business Rules

At its basic level of description, a *business rule* is simply a statement of Boolean logic.
Let's demonstrate this with a simple English example of a rule:

IF the car is low on gas **THEN** turn on the low-fuel light.

The rule as a whole is an IF/THEN evaluation, in which an appropriate action is taken based on the Boolean answer of true.

As you work with the BRE, you'll find yourself consistently designing with yes/no logic and acting on the resulting value.

Forward-Chaining Processes

Another interesting aspect of the BRE is the concept of forward-chaining logic processing. But don't get too worried over the terminology, as it's not as complicated as it sounds.

When working with rules, it's quite possible that the actions that you take with one rule may "activate" the situational logic of another rule. We call this a forward-chaining process because the events considered are all linked together. For instance, suppose that the following customer order is submitted to your e-commerce system:

```
<CustomerName>Dan Woolston</CustomerName>
<ProductOrdered>1882882</ProductOrdered>
<QuantityDesired>1</QuantityDesired>
<OrderStatus>O</OrderStatus>
<ProductPrice>19.99</ProductPrice>
```

The order comes in, and your system discovers that you do not have this product in stock. As you check the `QuantityDesired`, the order becomes back-ordered. So you'll change the `OrderStatus` to B, for back-ordered. You also have a rule in the system that says that any order with a status of B qualifies for a 5% discount, in accordance with your company's online availability guarantee.

The BRE will continue to evaluate a message until all of the rules have been satisfied.

On the first pass, the file will appear as shown previously. On the second run, it will look like this:

```
<CustomerName>Dan Woolston</CustomerName>
<ProductOrdered>1882882</ProductOrdered>
<QuantityDesired>1</QuantityDesired>
<OrderStatus>B</OrderStatus>
<ProductPrice>19.99</ProductPrice>
```

As the `OrderStatus` has changed, a final rule will process and modify the `ProductPrice` to reflect the guarantee:

```
<CustomerName>Dan Woolston</CustomerName>
<ProductOrdered>1882882</ProductOrdered>
<QuantityDesired>1</QuantityDesired>
<OrderStatus>B</OrderStatus>
<ProductPrice>18.99</ProductPrice>
```

After all of the appropriate business rules have run their course, your message is ready for action.

What's really cool about the BRE is that the business policies that you'll build are interchangeable. You don't need to shut down BizTalk processes to update the necessary components. As you deploy a new business rule, BizTalk recognizes that a new version has been implemented and it will pick up the new data.

Before we jump into the rule-creation process, let's take a look at the tool you'll be using to work this magic.

Introducing the Business Rule Composer

You'll find the Business Rule Composer, shown in Figure 12-3, in your BizTalk programs group under the Start menu. The Business Rule Composer is the utility that you'll be using to define your various rules, and you'll find it to be a very intuitive application.

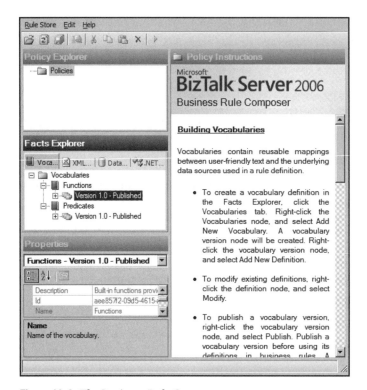

Figure 12-3. *The Business Rule Composer*

The Composer has four primary windows: Policy Explorer, Facts Explorer, Properties, and Policy Instructions.

Policy Explorer

You'll create your top-level policies from within the Policy Explorer. If you right-click Policies, you'll find just a single option, Add New Policy, as shown in Figure 12-4.

Figure 12-4. *The Policy Explorer*

You'll work with the Policy Explorer, momentarily, so let's continue with the other components of the Composer.

Facts Explorer

You've undoubtedly noticed that the Facts Explorer consists of four unique tabs, each representing the individual tools used to construct a BizTalk rule. Essentially, *Facts* are the building blocks of business rules. And as you can see in the Facts Explorer, you have access to powerful building blocks.

Let's take a quick look at each tab in this window.

Vocabularies Tab

The Vocabularies tab, shown in Figure 12-5, allows you to create and access Vocabularies. When you create Vocabularies, you are declaring that a set of terminology is representational of some form of logic. You can think of a BizTalk Vocabulary as being similar in nature to a function or variable name. The name itself is simply a pointer to a deeper set of functional data.

Figure 12-5. *The Fact Explorer's Vocabularies tab*

In BizTalk, you can assign real-world, meaningful nomenclature to the back-end processes. But why would you do that? One of the coolest features of the Business Rule Composer is that it can be used by nondeveloper, business-type analysts. By simply relying on the Vocabularies that you create, business analysts can construct business rules, without needing a deep understanding of BizTalk Server. Creating dynamic rules almost becomes a drag-and-drop experience for the business user.

XML Schemas Tab

The XML Schemas tab, shown in Figure 12-6, allows you to base your constructive Fact on data within an XML node. A front-end Vocabulary can be created to represent the embedded XML with minimal effort.

Figure 12-6. *The Fact Explorer's XML Schemas tab*

As you can see in Figure 12-6, I've added a sample XML schema to the Facts Explorer. Based on that addition, I could now use the schema nodes to create a unique rules process.

Databases Tab

As you might have guessed, the Databases tab allows you access to tables, wherein you may continue to build Vocabularies based on the information stored on the server. Figure 12-7 shows a sample database (AdventureWorks), ready for implementation.

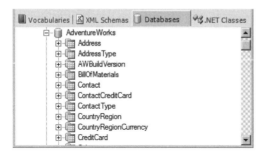

Figure 12-7. *The Fact Explorer's Databases tab*

.NET Classes Tab

It's my opinion that the .NET Classes tab is perhaps the most powerful of the group. With it, you'll be able to build intricate logic enforcement, based on customized .NET code. In the example shown in Figure 12-8, I've created a simple class, added it to the Global Assembly Cache (GAC), and referenced it from the Business Rule Composer. If you step back and think about what you could do with this kind of functionality, you'll see the incredible power that it gives your BizTalk processing.

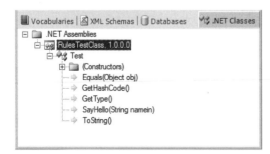

Figure 12-8. *The Fact Explorer's .NET Classes tab*

Properties Window

As expected, the Composer's Properties window is the typical property interface for the various components selected in the other Composer windows. Figure 12-9 shows an example of this window displaying the properties of an XML schema.

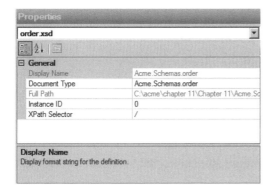

Figure 12-9. *The Properties window*

Policy Instructions Window

The Policy Instructions window is where a majority of your rule-creating labor will be spent. And most of that work involves simple drag-and-drop manipulation of the various Facts that you've created (or loaded). Figure 12-10 illustrates a simple policy in this window.

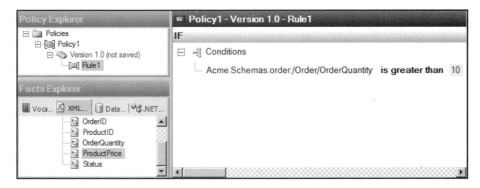

Figure 12-10. *The Policy Instructions window*

You now have a better understanding of the Business Rule Composer, and so it's a good time to make proper use of the tool by building your first rule.

Implementing a Business Rule

To demonstrate business rules, you'll need a simple orchestration-based application to use as a test harness. You'll build that first, and then add the rules.

Creating a Business Rule Application

First, in preparation of the project assembly that you will shortly undertake, create a directory to work within: `c:\acme\chapter12`. Within this folder, create two folders as you have in previous chapters: `c:\acme\chapter12\in` and `c:\acme\chaper12\out`.

You'll also be using a simple XML file for processing:

```
<Customer>
<Name>Dan</Name>
<Balance>90</Balance>
<Discount>0</Discount>
</Customer>
```

Create this file and save it as `customer.xml` in the `c:\acme\chapter12` folder.

Setting Up the Project Files

Now you're ready to set up the necessary project files. Because you'll be dealing with just a few files, you'll add everything to your new project.

1. Start Visual Studio 2005 and create a new, empty BizTalk project, saving it in the `c:\acme\chapter12` folder as `Chapter12Demo`.

2. Right-click the project name and add and generate a schema, as you've done in previous chapters. Use the `customer.xml` file as your well-formed XML base for the new schema. Save the schema as `customer.xsd`.

3. Change the data types of `Balance` and `Discount` to `xs:Decimal`. Your new schema should look like Figure 12-11.

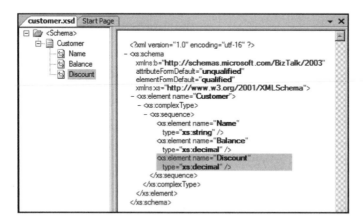

Figure 12-11. *The Customer schema*

4. Right-click the project name again and add a BizTalk orchestration, saving it as `RulesOrchestration.odx`.

You have all of the necessary files to complete the application, so let's turn our attention to the orchestration.

Creating the Orchestration

As you can imagine, you'll be using the `customer.xsd` file as the basis for your activity in this application. As in the previous chapters, you'll build the orchestration in the Orchestration View window.

1. Right-click Messages and select New Message.

2. In the Properties window of the message, change the Identifier property to `Customer`.

3. In the Message Type drop-down list, find the `Customer` schema that you added to the project earlier.

4. Drag a Receive shape out onto the design surface of the orchestration.

5. In the Properties window for the Receive shape, modify the following settings:

   - Activate: `True`

   - Message: `Customer`

   - Name: `ReceiveCustomer`

6. Under the Receive shape, place a Send shape and modify the following settings in the Properties window:

   - Message: `Customer`

   - Name: `SendCustomer`

7. Right-click the leftmost port surface and select New Configured Port. When prompted, name the port `ReceivePort` and the port type `ReceivePortType`. This will be a receiving port, and the port bindings will be specified later.

8. Connect the `ReceivePort` shape to the `ReceiveCustomer` shape.

9. Right-click the rightmost port surface and select New Configured Port. Name the port `SendPort` and the port type `SendPortType`. This will be a sending port, and the port bindings will be specified later. Your orchestration should look like Figure 12-12.

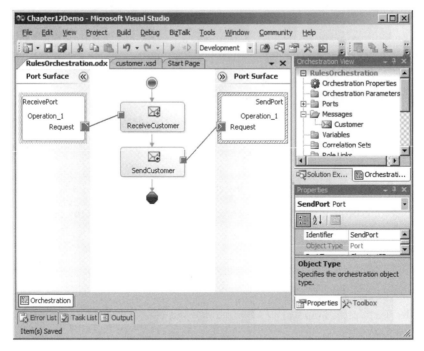

Figure 12-12. *The first stage of the orchestration*

Deploying the Application

Before continuing with the business rules portion of this example, let's build and deploy the application.

1. Add a strong name key to the project and set the deployment application name before deploying (a huge "gotcha"), as you have done in previous chapters.

2. Deploy the application to BizTalk Server and minimize Visual Studio.

We'll come back to the IDE in a few minutes to work on the business rule implementation.

Binding the Ports

As usual, now you need to bind the physical ports to the orchestration ports.

1. Start the BizTalk Server 2006 Administration Console.

2. Expand your new application and create the receive port and location as follows:

   - RulesReceivePort as the name of the one-way receive port

   - RulesReceiveLocation as the name of the receive location

   - File as the transport type (*.xml), configured to the c:\acme\chapter12\in folder

   - XMLReceive as the receive pipeline

3. Click OK when you're ready to continue.

4. Create the send port as follows:

   - RulesSendPort as the name of the static, one-way send port

   - File as the transport type, configured to the c:\acme\chapter12\out folder

   - PassThruTransmit as the send pipeline

5. Click OK to finish.

6. Open the Orchestrations folder for your application and bind the respective ports as shown in Figure 12-13 (don't forget to set the host):

   - ReceivePort to RulesReceivePort

   - SendPort to RulesSendPort

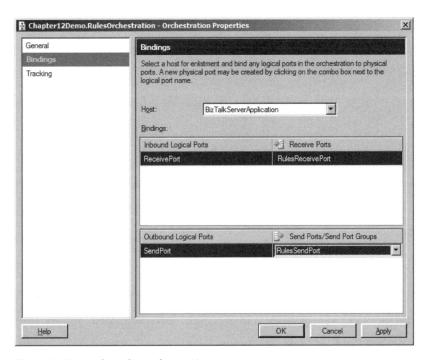

Figure 12-13. *Binding the orchestration*

Starting the Application

One of the shortcuts available, which we discussed briefly in Chapter 11, is the ability to start all of the ports and the orchestrations at the same time. BizTalk is smart enough to enlist and start things in order. If you right-click the application name in the Administration Console and select Start, you'll have a pop-up window dedicated to just this task. Click the Options button, and you'll see that BizTalk will let you pick and choose what you really do want to start, as shown in Figure 12-14. Here, you're interested in a do-all start, so just click Start to continue.

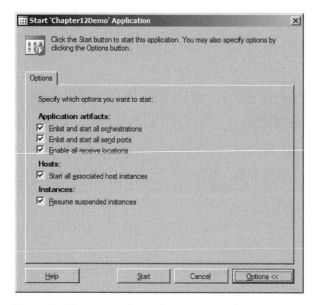

Figure 12-14. *Starting the orchestration application with one click*

If you click through all of the application components, you'll find that they have indeed started as expected.

And now for the moment of truth (for the first half of the application anyway)!

Create a copy of the customer.xml file and drop it into the c:\acme\chapter12\in folder. After a moment, BizTalk will pick the file and consequently drop a new file into the c:\acme\chapter12\out folder. If your computer is as pokey as mine is, you'll need to wait a moment or two before the file appears in the out folder.

So with a successful test, you now have the basic application waiting for you to add the business rules functionality.

Creating a Business Rule

You'll be creating a new rule, using the customer.xsd schema as the basis for decisions. You'll need the Business Rule Composer in order to complete this step, so start it up. As noted earlier, you'll find that in the BizTalk Server 2006 programs group in your Start menu.

Creating a Policy

One of the coolest features of business rules, in general, is the fact that you can create and update your rules, and BizTalk will handle the implementation of the newer processes for you. Another interesting opportunity that you have with BizTalk is that you can access a specific rule version through the API, if you have different versions of the same rule.

In this current example, you'll need to add a new rule, and you'll use the existing Version 1.0 that BizTalk provides automatically.

1. In the Policy Explorer window, right-click Policies and select Add New Policy. You'll notice immediately that the Policy name (Policy1) has become editable. Change the name to Chapter12Policy, as shown in Figure 12-15.

Figure 12-15. *Adding a new policy*

2. One of the first points of interest with the policy-creation process is the idea that all rules are versioned. Right-click the Chapter12Policy node, and you'll see the option to add a new version, as shown in Figure 12-16. We're not adding a new version at the moment, so click off the menu to close it.

Figure 12-16. *Policy options*

3. Right-click the Version 1.0 node and select Add New Rule.

4. Name your new rule Chapter12Rule.

In the pane to the right, you'll find that you've been provided a bit of an editor where you can build your rule, as shown in Figure 12-17. It's pretty lightweight, which is perfect for the amount of work that is required.

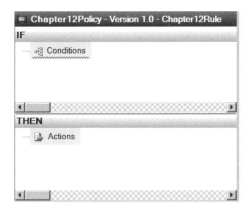

Figure 12-17. *Rules editor*

And this brings us to another rules concept that I mentioned earlier: Business rules are Boolean objects. Regardless of what data you're working with and how you manipulate it, the rule itself needs to evaluate to true or false. Based on that logic, you'll take a corresponding action within the THEN block. You'll see this in action in just a moment, but first you'll need to add your schema as a source for the rule.

Adding a Schema

The customer.xsd schema will become a Fact that you'll use in making your decisions. To put it very simply, business rules are decisions based on Facts.

1. Click the XML Schemas tab in the Facts Explorer.

2. Right-click the Schemas node and select Browse.

3. Locate the customer.xsd schema file and click OK.

4. Expand the Customer schema so that all nodes are visible, as shown in Figure 12-18.

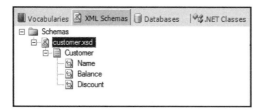

Figure 12-18. *The added Customer schema*

Adding the Logic

The Customer schema is now available as a Fact, and you can base decisive logic on the individual nodes. Before you work with those nodes, however, you need to have the decisive logic itself in place. As you can see in the IF/THEN panels, you have only condition and action points. If you right-click the Conditions tag, you'll have access to the various predicates that BizTalk has made available, as shown in Figure 12-19.

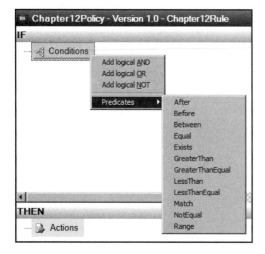

Figure 12-19. *Available rules predicates*

For the rule that you are developing, you want to modify the value of the customer's Discount node based on the current Balance. For customers with a low balance, you would like to encourage them to purchase more, by offering a larger discount on their transactions. The worded logic would be as follows:

IF the customer's **Balance** is **Less Than** 100 **THEN** the **Discount** should equal 10%.

The first task is to add the predicate for this business requirement. After you have a decision to make, you'll bring your customer Facts into the mix. Finally, to complete the full Boolean cycle, you'll add your corresponding action.

1. Right-click the Conditions tag and add a LessThan predicate, as shown in Figure 12-20.

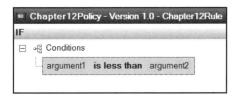

Figure 12-20. *Adding the LessThan predicate*

2. From the Facts Explorer, drag the Balance node out to the argument1 section of the predicate and drop it into the equation.

3. Click the argument2 element of the predicate and type the number 100. And that's it for the predicate consideration of the rule! It should look like Figure 12-21. Your rule has declared that you're going to take action based on the customer's balance.

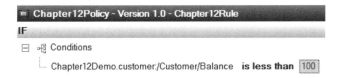

Figure 12-21. *The completed predicate*

4. Drop the Discount node from the Facts Explorer onto the Actions tag in the THEN panel, as shown in Figure 12-22. You'll notice that BizTalk recognizes that you're taking an assignment action, and so it will add the appropriate sentence structure for you.

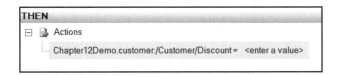

Figure 12-22. *Adding the action*

5. To add the `Discount` value, click the `<enter a value>` element and type the appropriate value: `.10`.

And you've successfully built the entire business rule for your orchestration!

Publishing and Deploying the Rule

For your rule to be available to the orchestration, you'll need to publish and deploy it to the server.

1. Right-click Version 1.0 of the policy, and you'll see that you have the option to Publish the rule, as shown in Figure 12-23.

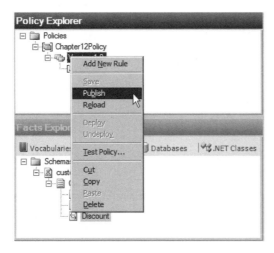

Figure 12-23. *Publish option for a business rule*

2. Click Publish, and allow the Business Rule Composer a moment to complete the action. Once the rule has been published, the version title will change to reflect the success of the request.

3. Right-click the Version 1.0 node again, and you'll see that you now have the ability to Deploy the rule. Select that option, and your rule will now be available for use! You can now close the Business Rule Composer.

Before we return to the orchestration portion of the application, I want to discuss an important caveat of the business rules process. Once you publish a rule, you *cannot* change it! You will need to distribute a newer version of the rule. Go ahead and try. Double-click the numeric values of your rule. You'll see that, indeed, they will not change. So before you roll out your rule, make sure that you're prepared to deal with the fact that it has become immutable at the point of publishing.

Adding the Business Rule to the Orchestration

Now it's time to return to your Visual Studio 2005 project. When you last worked with the project, you deployed a simple message-in/message-out application. You're now going to introduce a business rule to the equation!

1. In Visual Studio 2005, bring up the `Chapter12Demo` orchestration, if it's not already visible.

2. From the toolbox, drag a Call Rules shape to the designer, dropping it between the `ReceiveCustomer` block and the `SendCustomer` block, as shown in Figure 12-24. As the red exclamation point indicates, you need to do some configuration.

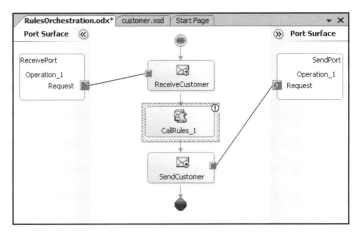

Figure 12-24. *Adding the Call Rules shape*

3. Switch over to the Properties window for `CallRules_1`, and you'll see that BizTalk is upset that you have yet to modify the Configure Policy property. Click the ellipsis for this property and select the business rule that you deployed.

4. Before you close the configuration window, you'll need to add the message as a parameter. After all, you need to give the BRE something to work with, right? Click the empty row within the parameter section, and your options will be crystal clear (there should only be one), as shown in Figure 12-25.

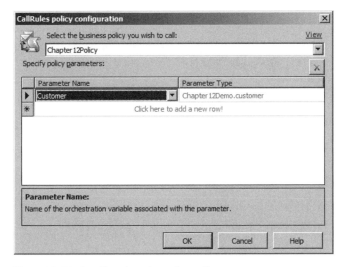

Figure 12-25. *Configuring the rules call*

5. Click OK after you have added the required parameters. Believe it or not, that's it! You have successfully added a business rule to your orchestration.

6. Save, build, and deploy this orchestration. You may want to stop and start the application within the BizTalk Administration Console, just to get a fresh start and to make sure that the orchestration and ports are still running.

7. Drop another `customer.xml` file into the `in` folder. After a moment, you'll find that the `out` folder contains the following:

```
<Customer>
<Name>Dan</Name>
<Balance>90</Balance>
<Discount>0.10</Discount>
</Customer>
```

Awesome! The BRE captured the XML message as a parameter, evaluated it, and then modified the `Discount` value as expected. You have officially built, published, and implemented your first rule!

Most of you, I'm sure, are now asking, "So is it true that I can change the rule logic, without having to redeploy or modify the orchestration?" Yes! Let's give that a shot, just to see it in action.

Updating a Business Rule

The company is feeling pretty generous of late, and now wants to give your good customers a 20% discount. You'll adjust the rule to accommodate the new requirement. As you know, you can't modify Version 1.0 of your `Chapter12Policy`. However, you can add another version of the component and deploy that instead.

1. Open the Business Rule Composer.

2. Right-click the `Chapter12Policy` node and select Add New Version. You'll receive a Version 1.1 that you can use for the update.

3. Drag-and-drop the `Chapter12Rule` from Version 1.0 to Version 1.1. This is a quick way to rebuild the previous rule. Of course, you could do a copy/paste operation, but the drag-and-drop method is faster.

4. You can now edit the fields. Go ahead and modify the `Discount` value to `0.20`, as shown in Figure 12-26.

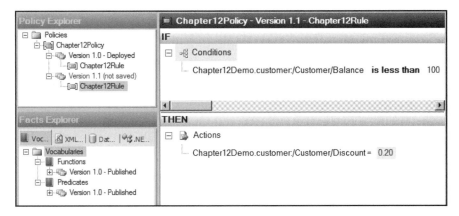

Figure 12-26. *The updated business rule*

5. Save, publish, and deploy the newer version of your business rule in the same manner as for the original version.

■**Caution** Remember that once you click Publish, that business rule is out there for keeps.

---

6. Drop another `customer.xml` file into the `in` folder, and watch as BizTalk works its versioning magic! As you check the file in the `out` folder, you immediately see that the new version has kicked in, and your `Discount` field has been modified:

```
<Customer>
<Name>Dan</Name>
<Balance>90</Balance>
<Discount>0.20</Discount>
</Customer>
```

Testing Business Rules

Another really interesting component of the Business Rule Composer is the ability to apply a test instance against your rule and see firsthand which rules are fired. Let's try it.

1. Right-click Version 1.0 and select Test Policy.

2. You're asked to assign a test instance for the Fact(s) being used by the rule, as shown in Figure 12-27.

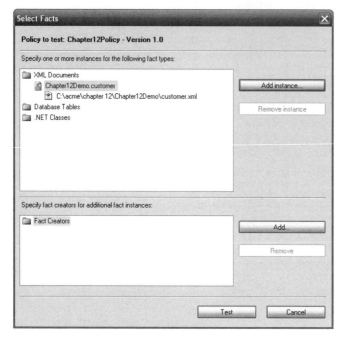

Figure 12-27. *Adding a test instance to the rule*

3. Add the test instance, and then click Test.

The BRE will process your rule. You'll also get a nifty report on the various rules and processes that were fired during the execution of your instance, as shown in Figure 12-28.

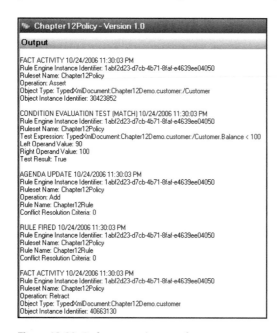

Figure 12-28. *Rules execution results*

Summary

Having the ability to update and test your business logic on the fly is, by far, one of the coolest aspects of the BizTalk Server platform. So much of what we deal with on the business side of things is dynamic and ever-changing. Having a platform from which we can deal with that in a fluid and easily updatable fashion is truly priceless.

I encourage you to dive deeper into the business rules world, as this simple demonstration only scratched the surface of what you can do with the Business Rule Composer.

In the next chapter, we'll take a look at the Business Activity Monitoring portal, also known as BAM. You'll have a chance to work with a tool that gives applicable visibility to what many would consider behind-the-scenes business processes on an end-to-end basis. That's quite a powerful ability when you really step back and think about it. A view of the enterprise from the comfort of a web page? Definitely!

CHAPTER 13

Business Activity Monitoring

Undoubtedly, you've come to realize by now that BizTalk is truly a powerful product. You've also seen how the various components allow you to create some pretty cool business processes. And if your company really embraces this product, you'll find yourself creating a *lot* of these really cool business processes. For a great deal of the implementations of BizTalk that exist out there in corporate land, BizTalk is responsible for a huge amount of end-to-end operational activity.

To help your business track all of this activity, BizTalk provides the Business Activity Monitoring feature. This chapter explains and demonstrates this functionality. But, like many of the features you've met in the previous chapters, BizTalk Activity Monitoring is a huge topic, which could fill a multitude of chapters. Again, I encourage you to continue with further study, following your work here.

What Is Business Activity Monitoring?

BizTalk can be the hub of a business architecture, responsible for orchestrating each step of the workflow. For instance, suppose that Acme, Inc. (the sample company we've been using throughout this book) had the order/fulfillment flow illustrated in Figure 13-1 (obviously, this is a very simplified rendition, and certainly more departments come in to play when a customer orders a product).

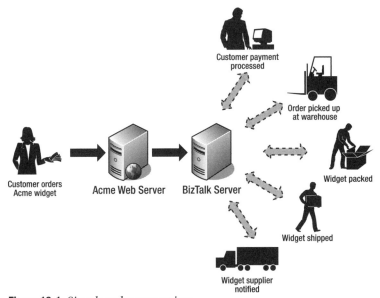

Figure 13-1. *Simple order processing*

As you've seen so far, building this type of application isn't terribly difficult. Technologically speaking, the application is pretty sound. Once it is built, the Acme orders start flooding in, with all departments reporting great success of the workflow implementation.

But then, the call comes in from your boss's boss, the head honcho. He commends you on a job well done and assures you that your hard work will certainly make him a much wealthier man. "But it sure would be great if our team of analysts could put some benchmarks against the various departments as they're working our Acme orders. Can you make that happen?" he asks. You notice that it isn't so much a question as it is a directive.

And the good news is that this ability is something you can certainly deliver. It's a part of the BizTalk Server application product called Business Activity Monitoring, or BAM for short.

But what is BAM? Is it a single application that you start and monitor in much the same way you do with the BizTalk Administration Console? Well, sort of.

We define BAM as a functionality of BizTalk. The BizTalk product provides the components necessary for us to implement process monitoring in whatever way the business user finds most comfortable. One of the most notable and often-used ways in which we do that is by leveraging Microsoft's Excel as the instrument of creation and presentation to the user. Business users can create their desired "wish list" of information that they would like to see represented in statistical form. The BizTalk developer will take this list, created in Excel, and use it as the basis for rendering the assets necessary for fulfillment of the request.

So in a nutshell, BAM is a facilitation product that connects the back-end business processes to the business user/analyst. We refer to this connection as *visibility*, as that term aptly describes what the product is trying to do. One of the more interesting points about this visibility is that it is not BizTalk-reliant. You could use the API from outside the application and have access to the necessary milestones and processes. In addition, there are web services available that allow you to call into BAM from other applications that are interacting with the data flow, providing access to the flow as a whole.

There are two important BAM components that we should examine first: activities and views.

BAM Activities

A BAM *activity* refers to the encapsulation and representation of an end-to-end process. This does not mean an instance of a single orchestration or messaging workflow. An activity could be a single process or a collection of many orchestrations or applications. A customer order workflow may involve a multitude of BizTalk orchestrations, with the message being bounced around from various corporate departments. The activity could simply be how long that order took to fulfill as a result of this complete work.

Within the activity definition, you generally find two entities:

- *Milestones* represent how long it takes to process something.

- *Data of interest* is made up of individual data points that you want to monitor (price, stock level, and so on).

By assembling the milestones and/or the data of interest, you collectively have a BAM activity.

BAM Views

A BAM *view* is a tailored representation of the data involved. If you've worked with SQL Server views, you'll have a head start on understanding the BAM view.

By implementing BAM views, you can disseminate your processes in a manner that is appropriate for the end user. For instance, you may have payroll logic for your accounting department that shelters the actual individual pay rates but presents the final cost of labor for a particular department.

With the definitions out of the way, it's time to try out BAM.

■**Note** In BizTalk Server 2006, you can also create BAM milestones and data of interest from within a Business Process orchestration diagram by using the Orchestration Designer for Business Analysts (ODBA). Fire up Visio and give it a try—when you're finished with this chapter.

Monitoring Processes

Before you begin with BAM, you need to have a BizTalk application up and running, so that you can feed it messages for testing purposes. For this example, you'll be using the application that you built in Chapter 11. If you skipped that chapter and the associated application, you'll need to return to it and build the application.

Drop a sample message (order.xml) into the appropriate OrderIn folder and ensure that you are indeed processing messages.

Specifying Monitoring Milestones

With the Chapter 11 application up and running, you're now ready to establish some basic monitoring milestones against the application.

Start Excel and ensure that you have the BAM plug-in listed in the toolbar, as shown in Figure 13-2.

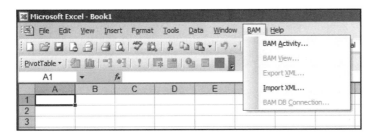

Figure 13-2. *The BAM plug-in for Excel*

If you don't have that menu option, click Tools ➤ Add-Ins ➤ Business Activity Monitoring. This will drop in the necessary BAM components.

For this example, you will track four milestones in relation to the Chapter 11 application. If you recall, the orchestration was rather simple, as shown in Figure 13-3.

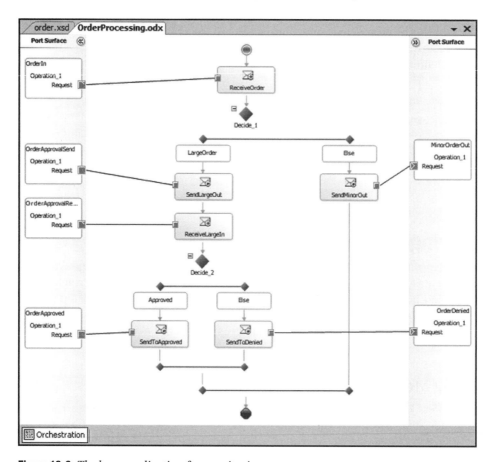

Figure 13-3. *The base application for monitoring*

As a business user (your role for this portion of the example), you are keenly interested in monitoring the points at which the data reaches its final destination, whether it's approved or denied. As you can see in Figure 13-3, those three events are the terminating points for the orchestration as well, so that will make this activity a bit easier to design.

Creating an Activity

With Excel running, you're ready to create an activity.

1. In Excel, click BAM ➤ BAM Activity. The Business Activity Monitoring Activity Definition dialog box appears, as shown in Figure 13-4. Click the New Activity button.

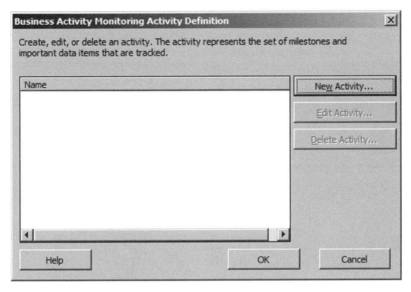

Figure 13-4. *Adding a new activity*

2. Name the new activity Chapter13activity.

3. As a business user, you know that you want to monitor the four events previously mentioned. Click the New Item button and add the following four items, each as a Business Milestones type:

   • OrderReceived

   • OrderApproved

   • OrderDenied

   • MinorOrderApproved

4. Your New Activity dialog box should look like Figure 13-5. Click OK to continue.

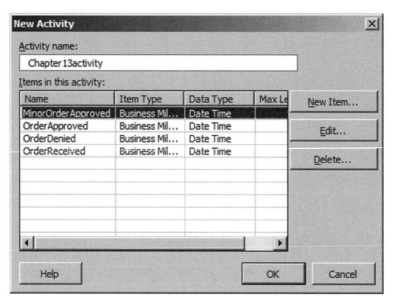

Figure 13-5. *The list of activity items*

5. Click OK in the Business Activity Monitoring Activity Definition dialog box to accept the creation of your first activity.

At this point, BizTalk will step in and guide you through the creation of a corresponding BAM view.

Creating a View

One of the coolest parts of the BAM View Creation Wizard is that you can select which milestones are appropriate for a particular view. You could create a view based on the same activity but present a different set of milestones for the individual business user.

An accounting department may be only interested in how long that message sat in that department waiting for approval, so that any inefficiency could be addressed. A corporate sales manager might be interested in knowing how long it takes the high-dollar orders to run through the entire approval process. The sets will both be based on the same activity, but they'll have access to different slices of information, courtesy of the BAM views. Both of these examples deal with service-level-agreement-type data. BAM can also show information like the total amount of orders received between certain times or grab data that can be analyzed in a cube, such as the values of the orders received by day, by item type, and so on.

As you continue with your view creation, you'll be asked to create dimensions and measures. A *dimension* is a description of the categories by which your aggregations will be grouped. BizTalk offers four dimension types: progress, data, time, and numeric range. For this example, you will use a progress dimension, which allows you to define stages and/or milestones that exist within a particular process.

A *measure* is an aggregation of items in your view. You have five choices for measure type: sum, count, average, maximum, and minimum. For example, you might want to distinguish the average time for order fulfillment. In this demonstration, you will apply a simple count measure.

1. In the Welcome dialog box, shown in Figure 13-6, click Next to start the view-creation process.

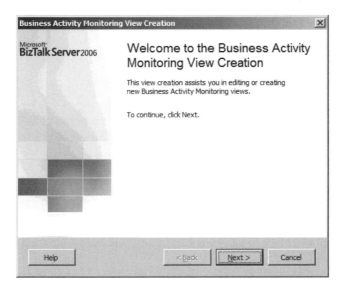

Figure 13-6. *The BAM View Wizard*

2. You'll be creating a new view, so select the appropriate setting (the only one, actually), as shown in Figure 13-7, and then click Next.

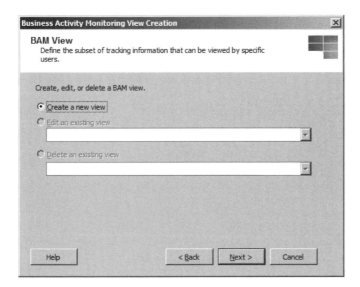

Figure 13-7. *Creating a new view*

3. You'll be asked to name the view, as well as specify the appropriate activities that you would like to associate with this view, as shown in Figure 13-8. You have only one activity, so one is all that's needed for this example. Pretty convenient, right? Click Next to continue.

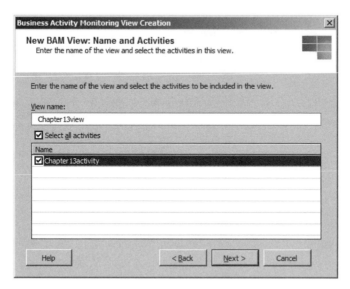

Figure 13-8. *Selecting the activity for the view*

4. You're asked to select the items for this view. For this example, select all four milestones, as shown in Figure 13-9. Then click Next.

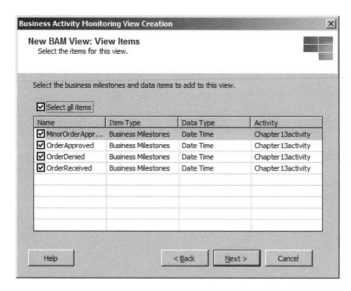

Figure 13-9. *Adding the milestones*

5. You're presented with the View Items/Management dialog box, shown in Figure 13-10, where you can specify an alias for the individual items. If you want to have something a little more legible than the current item names, you could certainly assign appropriate aliases here. However, for the purposes of this demonstration, you'll accept the named items and simply click Next to continue.

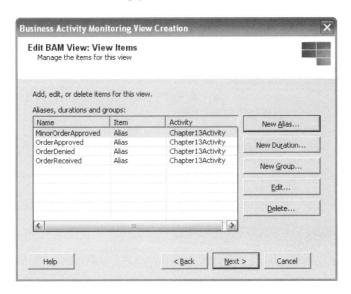

Figure 13-10. *The list of items for the new view*

6. In the Aggregation Dimensions and Measures dialog box, click the New Dimension button. Name the dimension Chapter13Dimension and accept the default type of Progress Dimension.

7. Click the New Milestone button. You'll need to add the corresponding milestone data, as shown in Figure 13-11, ensuring that you select the correct business milestone that is representative of the stage that you are creating here. Later on, you'll tie the milestones into your various orchestration steps, so that the milestones will represent the completion or arrival at the various stages.

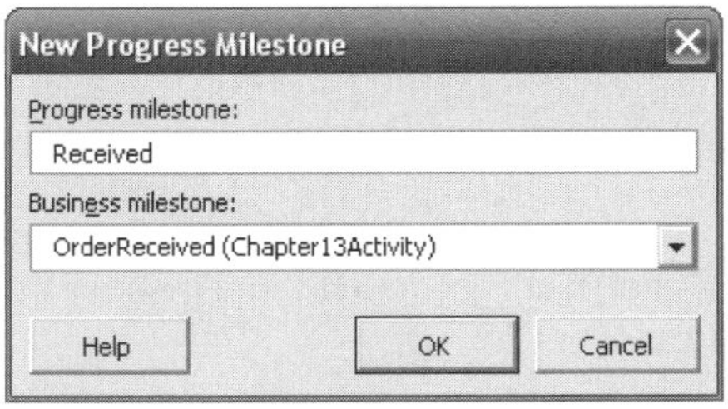

Figure 13-11. *Adding a new milestone*

8. Click the New Stage button and add the corresponding child stage to the milestone, as shown in Figure 13-12.

Figure 13-12. *Adding the first stage of the milestone*

9. Add three new milestones to the dimension by clicking the New Milestones button and assigning the logical business milestone to the progress milestones list. Figure 13-13 shows the completed dimension. Click OK to return to the Aggregation Dimensions and Measures dialog box.

Figure 13-13. *The completed dimension*

10. Click the New Measure button. Name the measure Count and select the Count radio button from the Aggregation Type list, as shown in Figure 13-14. You'll notice that the activity is chosen for you, as there is only one.

Figure 13-14. *Adding a simple measure*

11. Click OK to exit the New Measure dialog box, and then click Next in the Aggregation Dimension and Measures dialog box to continue.

12. Excel will now summarize the new view options that you have chosen, as shown in Figure 13-15. Click Next to generate the view.

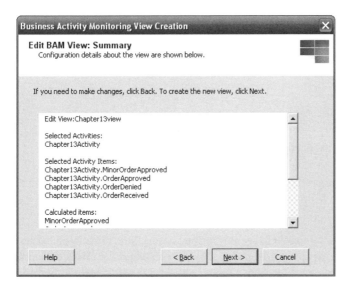

Figure 13-15. *The new view summary*

Your new view will now be instantiated, and a Pivot Table and associated grid will be laid out in Excel, as shown in Figure 13-16.

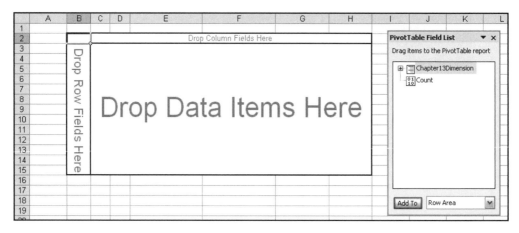

Figure 13-16. *The new Pivot Table and grid*

Setting Up the BAM Spreadsheet

You need to drop your data onto the grid, to set up how you would like to see the data represented.

1. Drag the Count aggregate out to the highlighted corner square. After you have dropped the Count, you'll notice that the grid will conform to a minimum display of the corresponding Count aggregate, as shown in Figure 13-17.

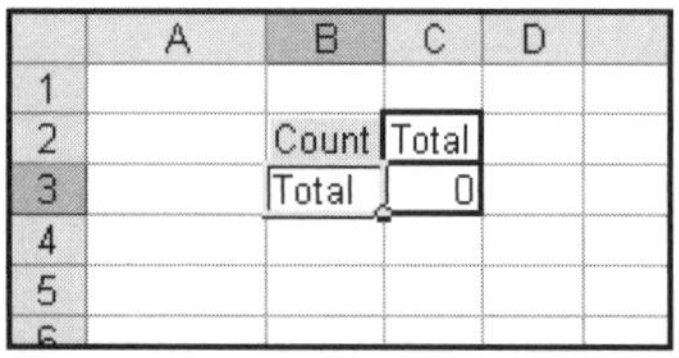

Figure 13-17. *Adding the Count aggregate*

2. Obviously, you're interested in a bit more information than just that, so drag out Chapter13Dimension from the Pivot Table Field List and drop it into the highlighted Total box.

3. You'll notice that you're unable to see the various stages that you created earlier. If you click the drop-down arrow on the header column, you'll find the check boxes you need, as shown in Figure 13-18. Check them and click OK. After adding the various stages, your new grid should appear as shown in Figure 13-19.

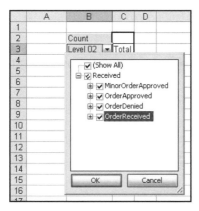

Figure 13-18. *Displaying the appropriate stages*

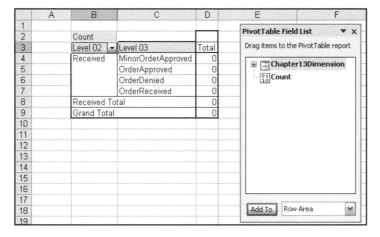

Figure 13-19. *The completed BAM spreadsheet*

4. To export the BAM spreadsheet to XML, click BAM ➤ Export XML in the Excel menu bar. Save your spreadsheet in the C:\acme directory, naming it ch13.xml.

5. Save the individual spreadsheet (c:\acme\ch13.xls), and then exit Excel.

Now you're ready to take off your business user hat and move on with the BAM process.

Deploying the Activity

Now it's time to assume the role of an IT worker who will receive notice from the business user that the necessary XML file has been created. Before handing the project off to the BizTalk developer, the IT worker needs to deploy the XML activity to the server. This can be done from the comfort of a simple command-line prompt.

Navigate to the BizTalk Tracking directory and enter the following command, as shown in Figure 13-20:

```
bm deploy-all -DefinitionFile:"C:\acme\ch13.xml"
```

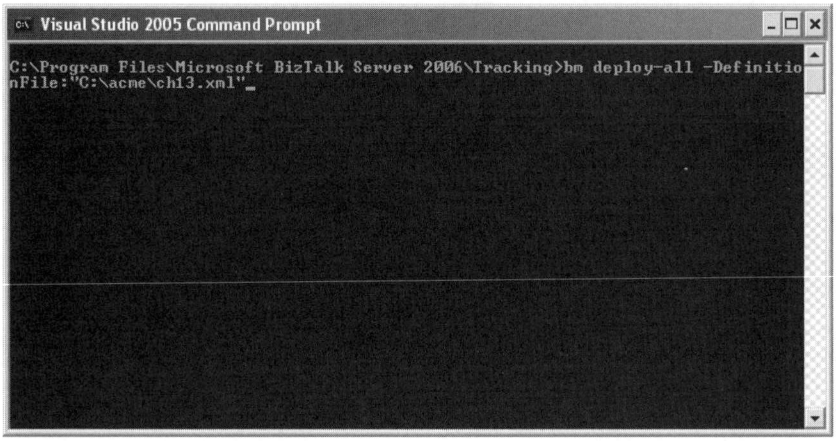

Figure 13-20. *Deploying the XML file*

After a moment or two, the XML file will have been deployed.

And now for the fun part! You take off the IT worker hat and move to the developer realm!

Creating a Tracking Profile

So far, you've had the business user tell you what kind of information he would like to track, and that definition has been made available as a resource to the BAM environment. However, you need to "map" the definition to some actual BizTalk activity. You'll accomplish that task with the BizTalk Tracking Profile Editor (TPE) application. You'll find that the TPE is a rather low-key application.

1. Start the TPE by clicking Start ➤ Programs ➤ Microsoft BizTalk Server 2006 ➤ Tracking Profile Editor.

2. When the program first starts, you have two choices: Import a BAM Activity Definition or Select an Event Source. Since you have a waiting activity definition, click on the appropriate link to import that.

3. Choose the Chapter13Activity definition, as shown in Figure 13-21, and click OK.

4. Now you need to add an event source to the TPE. If you think about it, what is the one thing that you're looking to track with this activity? If you guessed the Chapter 11 orchestration, then you would be correct. Back in the main TPE window, click the link to add an event source. Add the Acme.Orchestration, and you'll find that both panes of the TPE now resemble Figure 13-22.

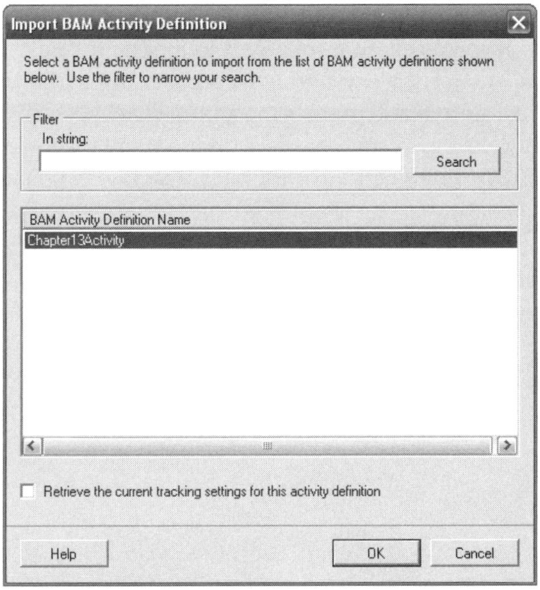

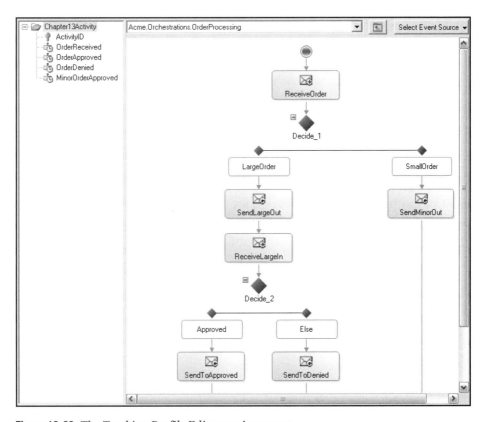

Figure 13-21. *Adding the activity definition*

Figure 13-22. *The Tracking Profile Editor environment*

5. To map the corresponding activity stages to the orchestration points, simply drag the shapes onto the activity stages. If you recall from your work in the Orchestration Designer, you dragged the send and receive ports from the port surface to the various shapes, so that they would be connected and process the appropriate messages. In the TPE, you drag-and-drop activity entities from the surface on the left to the indicated orchestration shapes. Map the following shapes to the `Chapter13activity` points:

   - `ReceiveOrder` shape to `OrderReceived`

   - `SendToApproved` shape to `OrderApproved`

   - `SendToDenied` shape to `OrderDenied`

   - `SendMinorOut` shape to `MinorOrderApproved`

   When you've finished, your activity list should look like Figure 13-23.

Figure 13-23. *The mapped activity stages*

6. Save your new profile as `ch13.btt` in the `c:\acme` directory.

7. On the menu bar, click Tools ➤ Apply Tracking Profile. And that's it—your process is now being monitored!

8. Drop some sample `order.xml` files into the appropriate application folders, as you did in Chapter 11.

Now that you have sent some messages through the approved, denied, and minor approved processes, you can take a look at the monitored results.

Using the BAM Portal

The BAM portal provides a very intuitive and easily accessible point of interaction for the BAM activities that you have created. Start it (click Start ➤ Programs ➤ Microsoft BizTalk Server 2006 ➤ BAM Portal Website), and you'll notice that you have the newly created `Chapter13view` as a selection, as shown in Figure 13-24.

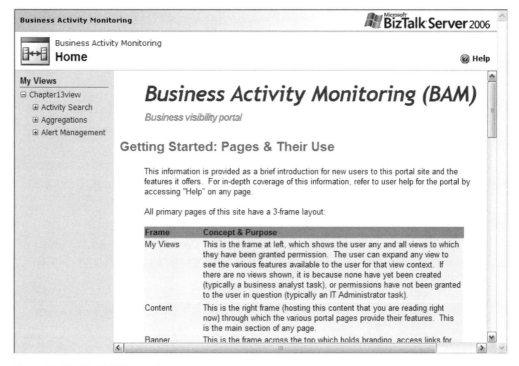

Figure 13-24. *The BAM portal*

And now let's take a look at some live data!

1. Click the plus sign next to Activity Search under your Chapter13New view.

2. Click the Chapter13Activity link to the left.

3. You can specify query parameters based on the activity stages that were established earlier. To do this, drag the necessary milestones over to the Items to Show box, as shown in Figure 13-25.

Figure 13-25. *Specifying the query parameters*

4. Click the Execute Query button, and you'll find that you have access to the orchestration data! Figure 13-26 illustrates the breakdown of the various messages that I've dropped into my orchestration and the corresponding milestones that were hit.

OrderReceived ▲	OrderApproved	OrderDenied	MinorOrderApproved
10/23/2006 9:27:29 PM			10/23/2006 9:27:29 PM
10/23/2006 9:27:52 PM		10/23/2006 9:28:05 PM	
10/23/2006 9:29:12 PM		10/23/2006 9:29:21 PM	
10/23/2006 9:29:40 PM	10/23/2006 9:30:00 PM		

Rows per page: 20

Figure 13-26. *Visibility of a business process*

5. Back in the main BAM portal window, click the plus sign next to Aggregations under the Chapter13New view. You'll see that you also have access to Pivot Table functionality, as shown in Figure 13-27.

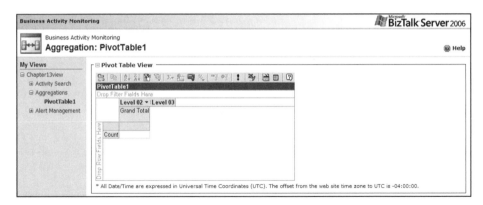

Figure 13-27. *BAM portal Pivot Table access*

As you may have guessed, the Chapter13view view is specific to the Chapter13activity activity. If you wanted to present a different view to another business user, you would need to revisit Excel and create a new view.

Summary

In this chapter, we've taken a cursory view of the BAM process. As I stated at the beginning of the chapter, there is *much* more to this topic. I encourage you to spend some time working with the Excel plug-in until you've become comfortable with creating customized business views. I also recommend that you investigate the BAM API and work with monitoring programmatically. As BizTalk Server 2006 picks up steam in the development world, I hope that we'll see more documentation and sample coding made available for BAM from other developers. As you work with this application and make discoveries of your own, please share with others what you have learned and help our community grow!

In the next chapter, we'll take a look at deployment. It's great that we can build these really cool messaging components, but if we're unable to move the projects out into the production environment, we will have worked for nothing. And so we'll explore the methodology behind deployment and take a look at some working examples.

CHAPTER 14

■ ■ ■

Application Deployment

During the course of this book, one of the things that we took for granted was the ability to deploy the various chapter applications with ease and little effort. If you've had the opportunity to work with BizTalk 2004 at all, you will have undoubtedly noticed that the process has become much more streamlined.

In the past, installing BizTalk processes was a laborious task that often left the developer with a headache and a fresh new resume on Monster.com. And I say "BizTalk processes" rather than BizTalk applications, because the concept of the application is new to BizTalk Server 2006. Previously, all of the artifacts that you needed to make a BizTalk orchestration or messaging process work would be thrown onto the server, and you would just do the best you could to decipher what went where. With BizTalk 2004 and Visual Studio as the "management" tool (using the BizTalk Explorer), you could organize your endeavors into Visual Studio projects; however, once they were deployed to the BizTalk Server environment, all bets were off.

As you have discovered, deploying via the application model is intuitive and something that we, as developers, find quite familiar.

In this chapter, we'll dive into the process of moving your application from the Visual Studio/design environment and out to the BizTalk Server environment. We'll begin with an architectural overview of typical BizTalk deployment models and also cover a few of the "gotchas" that tend to rear their ugly heads during the deployment life cycle.

The Application Model

With your orchestrations, ports, schemas, and other artifacts all encapsulated into an Application model, BizTalk provides a great deal of managerial benefits when it comes to updating, starting, and shipping your software. With BizTalk 2004, simply deploying and starting a messaging/orchestration process could sometimes create frustration on the part of the poor guy assigned to that task. If dependencies (like schemas and ports, for example) were not deployed and started in a specified order, chaos would ensue. Deployment chronology nearly became an art form rather than a BizTalk feature. Fortunately, BizTalk Server 2006 has addressed that issue, and I think that you'll agree that the experience is a huge improvement. You do still have a bit of homework to accomplish, however, before you deliver your awesome applications out to the enterprise.

If you'll recall, after building the various chapter components, you ran through a few steps prior to deploying the various artifacts to BizTalk:

- You needed to provide a strong name key for the application, through the Assembly properties, as shown in Figure 14-1.

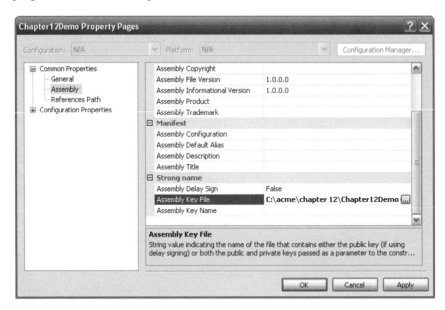

Figure 14-1. *Adding a key for deployment*

- You specified the application name for deployment, requested that the application be delivered on a redeploy basis (overwriting existing artifacts), and ensured that your host instance would be restarted after delivery. These items were set through the Deployment properties, as shown in Figure 14-2.

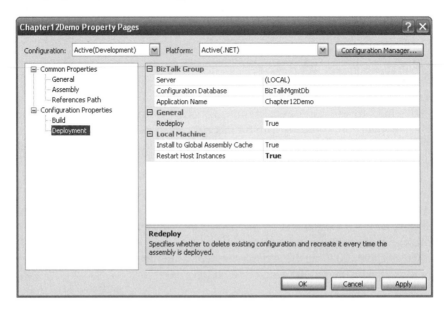

Figure 14-2. *Adding the deployment properties*

By specifying these preferences on a project basis, you're free to implement a simpler deployment process. You simply click the Deploy menu item. Then you can move on to more important tasks (testing and refactoring).

■**Note** The context of this deployment methodology is applicable to the work you're doing here in the book. I'm sure that many of you will be working with enterprise-level configurations, and that will change the deployment cycle for you. I don't want to overwhelm you with all of the processes involved in a large-scale application rollout, but I encourage you to pick up *Pro BizTalk 2006* (Apress, ISBN: 1-59059-699-4) as your next step in deployment education.

Once the application has been deployed, you're able to work with the components in a structured environment, with visibility into each of the application entities, as shown in Figure 14-3.

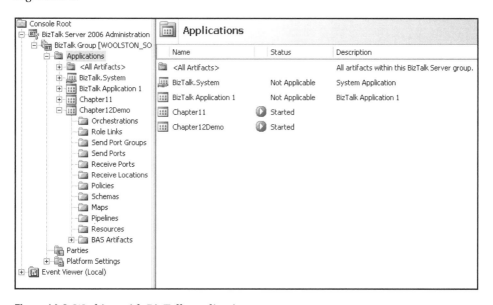

Figure 14-3. *Working with BizTalk applications*

As you've seen in earlier chapters, you can start a BizTalk application by simply right-clicking the application name in the Administration Console and requesting Start. BizTalk will handle the rest, and your awesome, world-changing application will be off and running.

And I can imagine that many of you are now saying, "Thanks for the review, but where are we going with this?" I have reintroduced our earlier process so that we can discuss the difference between deployment and staging.

Deployment

When you deploy an application (as you have many times over now), you are moving the resources necessary for functionality from the development tool to an instance of the BizTalk host. As you saw in Figure 14-3, BizTalk provides the application model, so you just need to get the resources in place and started. One of the "gotchas" that you may have come across during application deployment is the case of the missing deployment. I've been had by this many times and I'm sure you will, too.

The Case of the Missing Deployment

You build the application, give it a strong name key, and promptly deploy to BizTalk. You fire up the Administration Console, and "Hey! Where's my handy-dandy application that I just spent all week working on??!!" You scratch your head and check Visual Studio to find the "Deployment Successful" message. What gives?

BizTalk Server 2006 provides an out-of-the-box default application in the Applications group, listed as BizTalk Application 1, as shown in Figure 14-4.

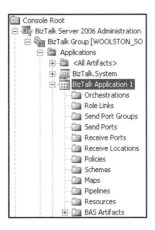

Figure 14-4. *Default BizTalk application*

Most likely, that's where your application has hidden. I typically will add the appropriate application name to the project properties, to avoid having this problem rear its ugly head. However, there is a way to relocate the files, should this happen to you.

Moving Application Objects

If your application has ended up in the wrong place, you can move it. Let's see how that works.

1. Right-click the existing Chapter12Demo application and complete a full stop of the application. Once the application has stopped, right-click the name again and select Delete.

2. Open the Chapter 12 solutions file. If you skipped the Chapter 12 application build but have another BizTalk application loaded and running, you can use that one.

3. Bring up the properties for the project and switch to the Deployment panel. Delete the application name listed, leaving it blank.

4. Build and deploy the application.

5. Open the BizTalk Administration Console and expand the BizTalk Application 1 folder. In the Orchestrations folder, you'll find your errant orchestration, as shown in Figure 14-5. Obviously, the default application is not where you intend to park your product. So let's create an empty application and move the orchestration and schema to their new home.

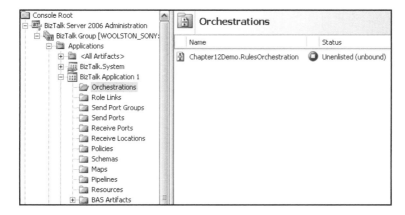

Figure 14-5. *The misplaced orchestration*

6. Right-click the Applications folder and select New ➤ Application, as shown in Figure 14-6.

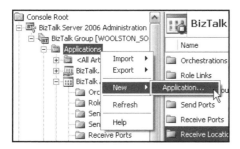

Figure 14-6. *Adding a new application*

7. Name your new application Chapter12Demo.

8. Now you need to move the files from the default application and into this new and improved location. Return to the BizTalk Application 1 folder and open the Orchestration folder, revealing the Chapter12Demo.RulesApplication orchestration.

9. Right-click the orchestration and select Move to Application, as shown in Figure 14-7.

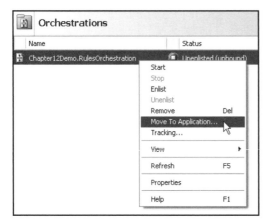

Figure 14-7. *Moving the components*

10. In the Move to Application dialog box, you're asked to specify the application to which you would like to direct your files. Select the Chapter12Demo entry. Notice that BizTalk recognizes that you have a few dependencies for the orchestration and decides to bring them along for the ride, as shown in Figure 14-8. Click OK to complete the move.

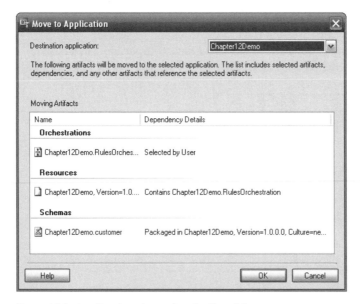

Figure 14-8. *Application dependencies listed for component move*

And now when you open the various folders in the default application, you'll find that the files have been relocated to the Chapter12Demo folder. You'll need to rebind the orchestration, if you plan to use the application for further testing.

After you've been bitten by the various deployment "gotchas" a few times, you'll find that your process will become nearly robotic: Key the app, name the app, and deploy. Obviously I'm generalizing, but I'll bet that you'll remember at least those few basic steps.

Staging

Staging is the act of shifting the deployed application from one environment to another. If your enterprise is anything similar to the pattern pictured in Figure 14-9, you'll have a keen understanding of what is typically known as the *migration path* for application development.

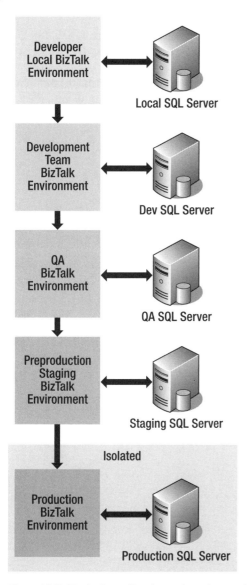

Figure 14-9. *Typical application migration path*

Whether you have fewer environments than those shown in Figure 14-9 or perhaps a couple more, the methodology is the same. As you test your applications, validate the functionality, and sign off on business requirement, you get closer to the production server where the application will go live to the world.

As you can imagine, having the developer change his project deployment settings to point to the appropriate migration stage is neither feasible nor recommended. What is recommended is the implementation of the application Microsoft Installer (MSI) process.

MSI Implementation

If you've worked with software for longer than a few minutes, you will have run across MSI technology. It's become somewhat of an industry standard for encapsulating and installing software. MSI files contain the resources necessary for product installation, and they add an associated entry to the Add/Remove Programs group. Fortunately, BizTalk Server allows you to export your existing application into an MSI file that you can use for installation on other servers, as you would any other software product. But how do you get your file?

There are two avenues that you can take to export your applications to the necessary MSI file: through the Administration Console or from the command line.

Exporting from the Administration Console

If you right-click the application name in the Administration Console, you'll find the ability to export to an MSI file listed, as shown in Figure 14-10.

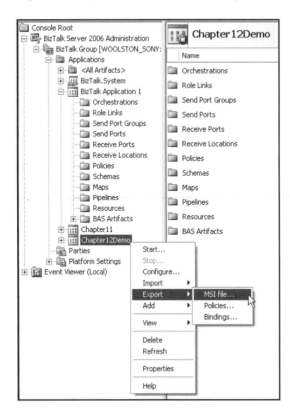

Figure 14-10. *Application export options*

Of great value is the fact that you're given a wizard to accomplish this task. As you step through the individual stages of the wizard, you find that you're able to include the various application resources for the MSI file, as shown in Figure 14-11.

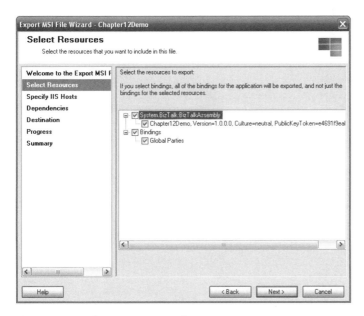

Figure 14-11. *Selecting resources for export*

If you had any virtual directories (IIS) that would have been included in the resource selection step, you would need to indicate IIS host information, as shown in Figure 14-12.

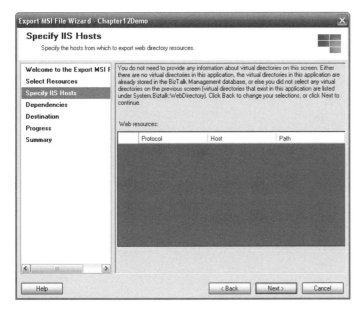

Figure 14-12. *Adding IIS host information*

One of the key ingredients of the wizard's success is that it informs you, ahead of time, what dependencies you'll need in existence on any box on which you'll be installing the current application. For instance, the sample `Chapter12Demo` application simply needs the BizTalk service running, as shown in Figure 14-13.

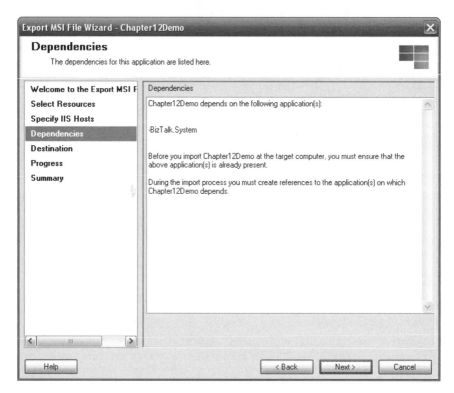

Figure 14-13. *Application dependencies*

You now need to specify the name that the application will install as on the destination machine. As expected, you'll need to also indicate where you would like your fresh new MSI file located after compilation. As you can see in Figure 14-14, I've asked to save it in an easy-to-remember spot.

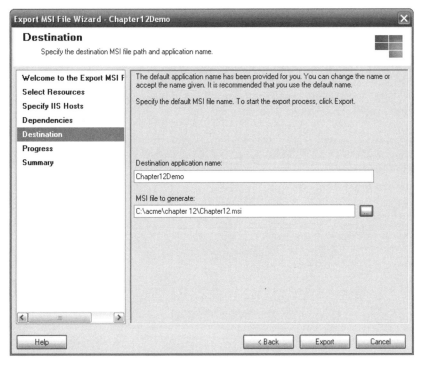

Figure 14-14. *Specifying the output MSI name and location*

Clicking Export will kick off the process, and consequently, you'll be met with the summation message.

You now have an installable version of the Chapter 12 application. And if you're like me, you instantly want to put the file to its intended use. Before you do that, let's delete the application from the Administration Console, so that you'll have immediate feedback of the successful run of the installation.

1. Delete the application from the Applications list as you did earlier.

2. Right-click the Applications folder and select Import ➤ MSI File, as shown in Figure 14-15.

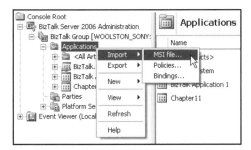

Figure 14-15. *Starting the import process*

3. As you would expect, one of the first tasks at hand is to indicate where your MSI file resides.

4. The next task is to specify the application that the prerequisite demanded. As you recall, BizTalk.System was deemed to be a dependency for your application. In this particular dialog box, you're given a list of available applications and asked to select the one that corresponds to that dependency. As you can see in Figure 14-16, BizTalk was kind enough to default that choice for you. Also of note is the Overwrite Resources check box. It does exactly what you think it does. If the application artifacts preexist, the installation process will overwrite them.

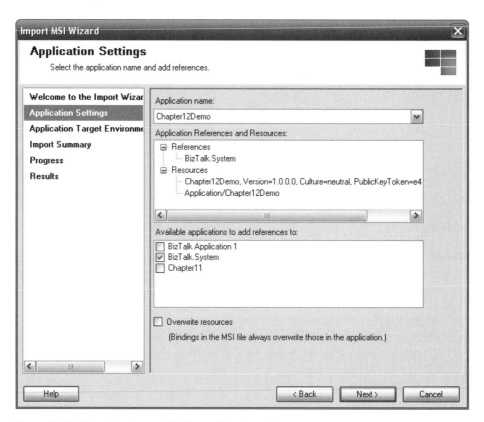

Figure 14-16. *Selecting the available application reference*

5. Because the existing server has only one staging environment (Default), you'll have but one selection choice in the next dialog box, as shown in Figure 14-17.

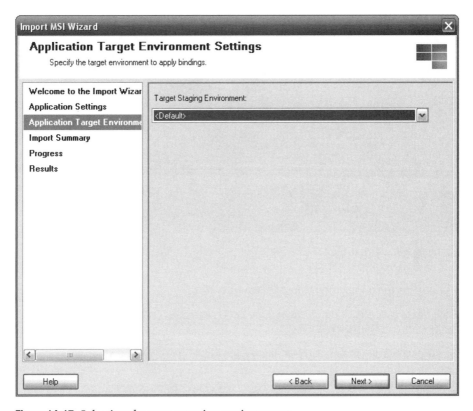

Figure 14-17. *Selecting the target staging environment*

6. The final step in the import process is the token summary screen. Click Import to run the wizard, and presto-change-o, you have a brand-new application in your application list!

You have successfully exported and imported a BizTalk application, with very little effort. But wait! Didn't I mention that there was another way to export and import an application? Yes, I did. The alternative to using the Administration Console's menu system to generate and consume the MSI file is the less-than-simple command-line interface, using the BTSTask utility. Why would anyone want to use anything other than the Administration Console? Well, imagine that you've automated your build and deployment process with scripting tools. Having the ability to deploy BizTalk applications from one stage to another via the command line suddenly becomes a viable methodology.

Using the BTSTask Command-Line Utility

A simple export command will move your application out to the MSI file:

```
BTSTask ExportApp -ApplicationName:Chapter12Demo
  -Package:C:\acme\Chapter12demoManually.msi
```

After a few moments, the BTSTask utility will process and deliver as anticipated, as shown in Figure 14-18.

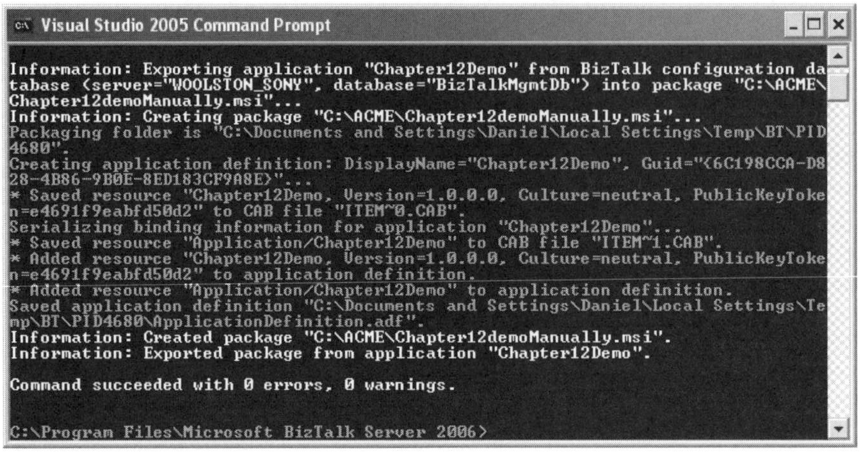

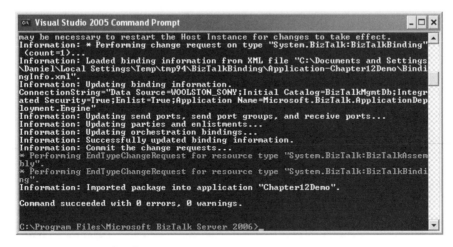

Figure 14-18. *Export complete*

Importing the application is just as easy:

```
BTSTask ImportApp /Package:C:\acme\Chapter12demoManually.msi
    /ApplicationName:Chapter12Demo
```

Again, BTSTask will process and deliver, as shown in Figure 14-19.

Figure 14-19. *Completed import process*

After running the process, Chapter12Demo is proudly present, waiting to be bound and started!

Advanced Deployment

I've entitled this brief section "Advanced Deployment" only because it deals with a couple of topics that you'll find to be a next step in your deployment education. As I mentioned earlier in the chapter, your future deployment endeavors will most definitely involve multiple environments existing on a variety of corporate servers. It's not unlikely that you will encounter development, quality assurance (QA), and production servers that will each have their own unique security settings, file structures, and more. Fortunately, deploying to different servers becomes less of a hassle with BizTalk Server 2006. Microsoft has provided two very important tools to help move things along in an orderly and expedient fashion: binding files and installation scripts.

Binding Files

When an application is stored in BizTalk Server, the corresponding artifacts (orchestrations, ports, and so on) are stored as entries in the BizTalk management database. A binding file is an XML representation of those entries, listing the interaction between the entities. You can use the binding file as a way of specifying, before deployment, what the various environment differences will entail for your application. You can modify the binding file to include settings for your development, QA, and production boxes, so that deployment becomes less tedious. To really understand the binding file, let's take a look at a sample from a previous chapter application:

1. Start the BizTalk Administration Console.

2. Locate a running application, preferably one of the more recent builds (Chapter 11 or 12).

3. Right-click the application name and select Export ➤ Bindings.

4. Specify an easy-to-find location for the XML file that will be generated. Accept the default binding settings and click OK to continue.

After a second or two, your new binding will be created. And let me warn you now: The file is huge. I'll demonstrate just a small amount of my Chapter 11 application binding file:

```
<?xml version="1.0" encoding="utf-8"?>
<BindingInfo xmlns:xsi="http://www.w3.org/2001/XMLSchema-instance"
 xmlns:xsd="http://www.w3.org/2001/XMLSchema"
  Assembly="Microsoft.BizTalk.Deployment, Version=3.0.1.0,
  Culture=neutral, PublicKeyToken=31bf3856ad364e35"
  Version="3.5.1.0" BindingStatus="FullyBound"
  BoundEndpoints="6" TotalEndpoints="6">
  <Timestamp>2006-11-21T00:06:35.3957953-05:00</Timestamp>
  <ModuleRefCollection>
    <ModuleRef Name="[Application:Chapter11]" Version="" Culture=""
        PublicKeyToken="" FullName="[Application:Chapter11],
        Version=, Culture=, PublicKeyToken=">
      <Services />
      <TrackedSchemas>
        <Schema FullName="Acme.Schemas.PropertySchema.PropertySchema"
        AssemblyQualifiedName="Acme.Schemas.PropertySchema.PropertySchema,
  Acme.Schemas, Version=1.0.0.0, Culture=neutral,
  PublicKeyToken=e4691f9eabfd50d2"
  AlwaysTrackAllProperties="false">
          <TrackedPropertyNames />
```

```
. . .
<ReceivePort Name="ApprovalSubmittedPort" IsTwoWay="false" BindingOption="1">
    <Description xsi:nil="true" />
    <ReceiveLocations>
      <ReceiveLocation Name="ApprovalSubmittedLocation">
        <Description xsi:nil="true" />
        <Address>C:\acme\chapter 11\ApprovalSubmitted\*.xml</Address>
        <PublicAddress />
        <Primary>true</Primary>
        <ReceiveLocationServiceWindowEnabled>
          false
        </ReceiveLocationServiceWindowEnabled>
        <ReceiveLocationFromTime>2006-10-23T04:00:00</ReceiveLocationFromTime>
        <ReceiveLocationToTime>2006-10-24T03:59:59</ReceiveLocationToTime>
        <ReceiveLocationStartDateEnabled>false</ReceiveLocationStartDateEnabled>
        <ReceiveLocationStartDate>2006-10-22T20:00:00</ReceiveLocationStartDate>
        <ReceiveLocationEndDateEnabled>false</ReceiveLocationEndDateEnabled>
        <ReceiveLocationEndDate>2006-10-23T20:00:00</ReceiveLocationEndDate>
        <ReceiveLocationTransportType Name="FILE" Capabilities="11"
            ConfigurationClsid="5e49e3a6-b4fc-4077-b44c-22f34a242fdb" />
```

As I've stated, this is only a small sampling of the complete file, but it's enough to demonstrate that you have an XML representation of your application here. With a few additions and changes, the file can be modified to allow for deployment to your other environments.

Processor Scripts

You'll remember that when you started a few of the sample applications, you needed to first create the physical file folder locations that you would use in conjunction with the application send and receive ports. Now imagine that you're deploying these same applications out to servers that don't have these directories in place. What would happen if you tried to run the application? You're right, it wouldn't work. Fortunately, within the BizTalk deployment process, you can indicate that additional steps must be taken to prepare the application for a successful startup. You do that through the use of preprocessing and postprocessing scripts.

Preprocessing Scripts

Sometimes you have housekeeping that needs to be taken care of before BizTalk starts building things on the server. Perhaps you need a few directories created or some .NET assemblies added to the Global Assembly Cache (GAC). You could do that through scripting. One of the more commonly used methods, .bat files, can be thrown together rather quickly and used to build directory structures as well as other script-based tasks.

After creating a .bat script, you add that as an artifact to the application itself by right-clicking the application name and selecting Add ➤ Preprocessing Scripts.

Postprocessing Scripts

After BizTalk has installed the application, you might have a list of jobs that will require the application to be in place before executing (starting orchestrations, ports, and so on). Or maybe you would like to do some cleanup work within a .bat file. All of that can be done through the postprocessing script process.

After creating the script, add the file to the application by right-clicking the application name and selecting Add ➤ Postprocessing Scripts.

Summary

As you've been reading through this chapter, you've probably been able to catalog a list of questions concerning deployment, staging, and BizTalk architecture in general. There is so much more to the technology than what we've covered in the scope of this book. Fortunately, a plethora of resources are available to help kick your BizTalk knowledge up to the next level. Once again, I encourage you to pick up *Pro BizTalk 2006* as your next step on the BizTalk path. It will undoubtedly complement your hard-earned business integration skills as you set off to save the world, one orchestration at a time!

Index

You Need the Companion eBook